Transactions
of the
American Philosophical Society
Held at Philadelphia
For Promoting Useful Knowledge
Volume 90, Pt. 5

ADAM HOOPS, THOMAS BARCLAY, AND THE HOUSE IN MORRISVILLE KNOWN AS SUMMERSEAT, 1764-1791

❦❦❦❦

Priscilla H. Roberts
and
James N. Tull

AMERICAN PHILOSOPHICAL SOCIETY
INDEPENDENCE SQUARE · PHILADELPHIA
2000

ISBN:0-87169-905-2
US ISSN: 0065-9746

Library of Congress Cataloging in Publication Data

Roberts, Priscilla H., 1935-
  Adam Hoops, Thomas Barclay, and the house in Morrisville known as Summerseat, 1764-1791 / Priscilla H. Roberts and James N. Tull.
    p.   cm. -- (Transactions of the American Philosophical Society, ISSN 0065-9746 ; v. 90, pt. 5)
  Includes bibliographical references and index. ISBN 0-87169-905-2 (pbk.)
      1.Summerseat (Morrisville, Bucks County, Pa.) 2. Morrisville (Bucks County, Pa.)--Buildings, structures, etc. 3. Morrisville (Bucks County, Pa.)--History-- 18th century. 4. Morrisville (Bucks County, Pa.)--Biography. 5. Hoops, Adam, 1709-1771-- Homes and haunts--Pennsylvania--Morrisville (Bucks County) 6. Barclay, Thomas, 1728-1793--Homes and haunts--Pennsylvania-- Morrisville (Bucks County) 7. Pioneers--Pennsylvania-- Morrisville (Bucks County)--Biography. 8. Washington, George, 1732-1799--Homes and haunts--Pennsylvania-Morrisville (Bucks County) 9. Pennsylvania--History--Revolution, 1775-1783. 10. Philadelphia (Pa.)--History--Revolution, 1775-1783. I. Tull, James N., 1920- II. Title. III. Series.

F159.M79 R63 2000
974.8'21--dc21

                                                                      00-065047

CONTENTS

List of Illustrations

INTRODUCTION

Summerseat is an eighteenth century Georgian manor house, owned and operated by the Historic Morrisville Society in Bucks County, Pennsylvania. It was saved from dereliction and decay twice in the twentieth century by the good citizens of Morrisville. The names changed, but the determination endured. They restored the crumbling building in the 1930s, arranged for a Pennsylvania Historical Marker in 1949, applied for National Historic Landmark status in 1971, incorporated as a non-profit society in 1976, and purchased the historic house in 1980.[1]

As a National Historic Landmark, Summerseat is recognized as having "exceptional value" to the history of the United States.[2] This seems something of an understatement, when we learn that Summerseat was not only the headquarters of General George Washington for a week in December 1776, but was also owned by four prominent Americans of the eighteenth century. Two of them, Robert Morris and George Clymer, are known and have been subjects of biographies, doctoral dissertations, and periodic scholarly attention.[3] Morris, Superintendent of Finance during the Revolution-

---

[1] Richard H. S. [G.] Osborne, "Historic 'Summerseat'," *A Collection of Papers Read Before the Bucks County Historical Society* (hereafter *Bucks County Papers*), 3 (1909), 237-42; Thomas B. Stockham, "Preserving 'Summerseat'," *Bucks County Papers*, 6 (1932), 53-57; George R. Beyer, *Guide to the State Historical Markers of Pennsylvania*, 5th ed. (Harrisburg, 1991), 13; U.S. Department of Interior, National Park Service, *National Historic Landmarks* (Washington, 1976), 117; William J. Murtagh, *The National Register of Historic Places* (Washington, 1976), 633; U.S. Department of Interior, National Park Service, *Catalogue of National Historic Landmarks 1987* (Washington, 1987), 227; *America Preserved: a checklist of historic buildings, structures, and sites* (Washington, 1995), 802-03; Deed of Purchase of Summerseat by Historic Morrisville Society, dated June 20, 1980, Bucks County Deed Book 2389, p. 726, recorded July 10, 1980; and Birgitta Nyholm, "Morrisville's historic Summerseat may go on the block," *Trenton Times*, May 28, 1976. We are greatly indebted to Betty Huber for some of these sources and dates.

[2] "Summerseat has been designated a Registered National Historic Landmark under the Provisions of the Historic Sites Act of August 21, 1935. This site possesses exceptional value in commemorating or illustrating the history of the United States. U.S. Department of the Interior, National Park Service. 1971." Bronze plaque on display at Summerseat.

[3] E. James Ferguson, John Catanzariti, Elizabeth M. Nuxoll, and Mary A. Gallagher, eds., *The Papers of Robert Morris, 1781-1784*, 9 vols. (Pittsburgh, 1973-1998); Ellis P. Oberholtzer, *Robert Morris, Patriot and Financier* (New York, 1903); A.M.

(continued...)

ary War, purchased Summerseat to add to his already extensive holdings in Morrisville.[4] Later George Clymer, prominent Phila-

---

[3](...continued)
Sakolski, "Robert Morris, Patriot and Bankrupt," *Nation's Business*, 18 (April 1930, no. 4), 36-38,202,204,206; Ellis P. Oberholtzer, "Robert Morris Founder of Morrisville," *Bucks County Papers*, 3 (1909), 345-355; Eleanor Young, *Forgotten Patriot Robert Morris* (New York, 1950); and William Graham Sumner, *Robert Morris*, (New York, 1892). A further forty-two citations are listed in the electronic version of Biography and Genealogy Master Index.

Jerry Grundfest, *George Clymer: Philadelphia Revolutionary, 1739-1813* (New York, 1982); James R. MacFarlane, *George Clymer Signer of the Declaration of Independence, Framer of the Constitution of the United States and of the State of Pennsylvania, His Family and Descendants* (Philadelphia, 1927); James Grant Wilson and John Fiske, eds., *Appleton's Cyclopaedia of American Biography* (New York, 1888) 1, 664-65; Allen Johnson and Dumas Malone, eds., *Dictionary of American Biography* (hereafter DAB), 21 vols (New York, 1928-1936); Walter H. Mohr, "George Clymer," *Pennsylvania History*, 5 (1938), 282-85; Ruth L. Woodward and Wesley Frank Craven, *Princetonians: 1784-1790* (Princeton, 1991), "Henry Clymer," 109-11, "Meredith Clymer," 176-78; and Nicholas B. Wainwright, *History of the Philadelphia National Bank: A Century and a Half of Philadelphia Banking, 1803-1953* (Philadelphia, 1953),7-9, 16-17, 20, 32, 34. For further information, the electronic version of Biography and Genealogy Master Index lists twenty source citations.

[4] Morris's land purchases in the Morrisville area were seven contiguous tracts of land in Pennsylvania and one in New Jersey, all fronting on the Delaware River:

1) 8 March 1787 - 383 acres and half "or near four hundred acres" bought from John Nixon;

2) 11 December 1789 -"the delaware Works," a dam, and "woods Island" totalling 450 acres from Samuel Ogden;

3) [Undated. 1790?] - 833 and a quarter acres, plus the six-acre Goat Island from the estate of Thomas Nichlin and wife;

4) 28 November 1791 - a second tract "called Summerseat...containing two hundred twenty one acres & eighty three perches..." bought from John Ashley, attorney for John Eddowes, Martin Petrie and William Ellis [creditors to Thomas Barclay];

5) 10 April 1792 - 50 acres containing a ferry to Trenton from John Borrows and John Seull;

6) 15 November 1792 - 264 acres and one quarter of an acre from Patrick Colvin;

7) 15 April 1793 - 110 acres from Benjamin Linton and Samuel Linton;

8) 18 September 1794 - land "at the falls of delaware near trenton known by the name of the Middle or old ferry situate in the township of Notingham in the county Burlington...containing seventeen acres and a quarter..." from Joseph
(continued...)

delphian and, like Robert Morris, a signer of the Declaration of Independence and of the U. S. Constitution, purchased the property and lived there intermittently with his son and family.[5]

Regarding the first two owners, Adam Hoops and Thomas Barclay, one finds no dissertations, monographs or even serious study.[6] It was Adam Hoops, born in 1709, who assembled the estate

---

[4](...continued)
  Borrows and wife Sarah.

Deed of Indenture between Robert Morris and wife and the President and Directors of the Insurance Company of North America, dated January 9, 1795, Bucks County Papers, Box no. 1, Historical Society of Pennsylvania (hereafter HSP); notice of sale in the *State Gazette and New Jersey Advertiser* (Trenton), June 5, 1798.

[5]George Clymer and Thomas Fitzsimmons, "as the highest & best bidders," purchased the Morris properties, including the Summerseat estate, at public vendue when Robert Morris's bankruptcy forced a fire sale of his Morrisville lands on June 9, 1798. Deed and Map of Mortgaged Lands of Robert Morris sold by sheriff Daniel Thomas, August 6, 1798, Bucks County Box Manuscripts, HSP. On March 20,1805 Clymer deeded the Summerseat property to his son Henry and wife Mary. Henry Clymer in turn sold 162 1/2 acres of the Summerseat estate to Henry L. Waddell and wife Elizabeth Pemberton Waddell on July 27, 1812. Deed of Indenture between Henry Clymer and wife Mary and John Wilson for Henry L. Waddell, dated July 27, 1812. Bucks County Deed Book 41, 234-36. See also the Deed of Release between Ebenezer Hazard, late Secretary of the Insurance Company of North America, and Thomas Fitzsimmons and George Clymer of October 3, 1803, Bucks County Deed Book 41, 232-33.

[6] Adam Hoops has not fared well by Bucks County historians. J. H. Battle does not mention him (*History of Bucks County Pennsylvania* (1887; Spartanburg, S.C., 1985), neither do contemporary historians Terry A. McNealy and George F. Lebegern, Jr. (*A History of Bucks County Pennsylvania*, Part 1, Fallsington, 1970, and *Episodes in Bucks County History: a Bicentennial Tribute, 1776-1976*, Doylestown, 1975). William W. H. Davis's three-volume *History of Bucks County, Pennsylvania from the Discovery of the Delaware to the Present Time*, 2nd ed.(New York, 1905), gives him a few lines (some incorrect) as owner of land in Lower Makefield township, but does not connect him to Summerseat (1:85). Dr. Richard H. G. Osborne, whose father-in-law owned Summerseat from 1860 to 1894, omits Hoops in the list of its owners (*Bucks County Papers*, 3 (1909): 237).

  Thomas Barclay and Summerseat fare somewhat better, though neither is mentioned by Battle. Davis includes a photograph of Summerseat in volume one and is the first author to identify it with Thomas Barclay, although he mistakenly names him as the builder, an error often repeated by subsequent writers. Although Davis put commendable effort into his history, much is anecdotal and therefore should be used with caution. He makes erroneous statements about Robert Morris, that he lived in Morrisville and resided at Summerseat, when no documentary evidence confirms that (2:117,164,168n). Davis is also mistaken when he writes that the heirs

(continued...)

piecemeal from land purchases in 1764, 1765, and 1766 (see Map 1 and Appendix E). Hoops, one of the important figures of the French and Indian War, named it Summerseat and made it his home. In 1773 his son-in-law, Thomas Barclay, bought it as his country seat. Barclay was one of America's early diplomats. Appointed by the Continental Congress in 1781, he was the first person ever to serve abroad as consul for the United States. It was during their ownership, from 1764 to 1791, that Summerseat saw its share of renown, especially during the American Revolution.

ADAM HOOPS

Adam Hoops is unknown to most Pennsylvanians today. But at the time of his death in 1771, he was one of the wealthiest men in the Province. Other than a few entries in the Colonial Records and Archives of Pennsylvania, Adam Hoops remains a mystery to most historians.[7]

---

[6](...continued)
of Adam Hoops sold the plantation in Lower Makefield to Daniel Clark, when it was Adam Hoops who purchased it and gave it to his daughter and son-in-law (1:85); when he writes that "the first mill at Morrisville was built in 1772-73, while the property was in the possession of the widow and sons of Adam Hoops," when the mills, built by Adam Hoops, were in existence at the time of his death in June 1771 (2:163); and when he writes that George Clymer died at Summerseat (2:164). Clymer did die at the home of his son in Morrisville, but was that home Summerseat? Henry Clymer sold Summerseat in July 1812. His father died in January 1813. (Nicholas B. Wainwright, *History of the Philadelphia National Bank*, 34). Henry Clymer had purchased three lots in 1804 "in the said Borough of Morrisville." (Deed of Indenture between Jesse Palmer and Henry Clymer of June 7, 1804 cited in Claim between Mary Clymer and Commonwealth of Pennsylvania for Delaware Division Canal damages to her property, June 14, 1834, in Record Group 17, Records of the Office of Land Records, Canal Commissioners Map Books, Book No. 42, p.48, Pennsylvania State Archives). Was one of these lots the farm on which Henry Clymer died in 1830? And where George Clymer died in 1813?

[7] Charles Henry Hart made an effort to find out who Adam Hoops was. "Notes and Queries," *Pennsylvania Magazine of History and Biography* (hereafter PMHB), 35 (1911): 512. Edward G. Williams came close, when he called him "one of the prodigies of the New World." *Bouquet's March to the Ohio: The Forbes Road. From the Original Manuscript in the William L. Clements Library*, edited with Historical Introduction, Notes, and Appendixes (Lancaster, 1975), 52n. Brief information on Adam Hoops can be found in Nelson Osgood Rhoades, ed., *Colonial Families of the United States of America*, 7 vols., (1907-1920; Baltimore, 1966), 7: 482-83, under

(continued...)

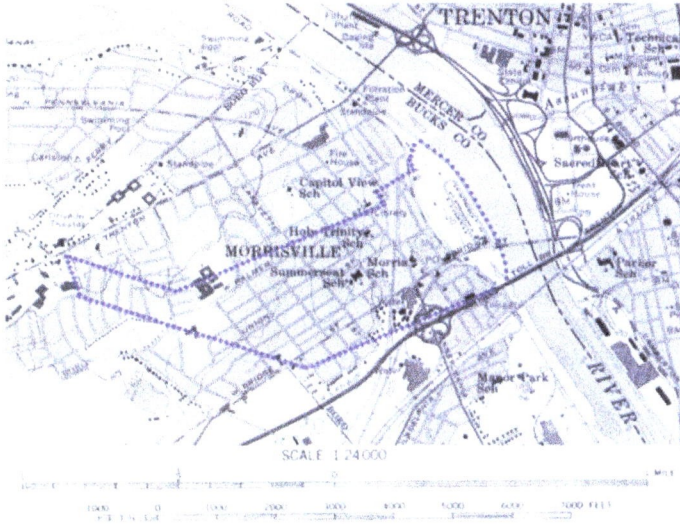

Map 1. The blue dotted line locates the original Summerseat estate on this 1981 map of Morrisville. US Geological Survey map, Trenton West Quadrangle (New Jersey-Pennsylvania) 1955, Photo revised 1981.

Of vague origins and unknown parentage,[8] Hoops appears first

---

[7](...continued)
"Watson."

Historians of colonial Philadelphia have overlooked Adam Hoops. There is no mention of him in the index to J. Thomas Scharf and Thompson Westcott, *History of Philadelphia, 1609-1884*, 3 vols., (Philadelphia, 1884), although Hoops's name is given as a signer of the Non-Importation Agreement of 1765 in 1:273; in Carl Bridenbaugh, *Cities in Revolt: Urban Life in America, 1743-1776* (New York, 1970); Carl and Jessica Bridenbaugh, *Rebels and Gentlemen: Philadelphia in the Age of Franklin*, (New York, 1962); Thomas M. Doerflinger, *A Vigorous Spirit of Enterprise: Merchants and Economic Development in Revolutionary Philadelphia* (Chapel Hill, 1986), or in Gary B. Nash, *The Urban Crucible: Social Change, Political Consciousness, and the Origins of the American Revolution* (Cambridge, MA, 1979). Robert F. Oaks cites Hoops in a table of merchants in his doctoral dissertation, "Philadelphia Merchants and the American Revolution, 1765-1776," (Univ. of Southern California, 1970), 224, where he is listed as an artisan.

[8] Research continues into Adam Hoops's antecedents. He was either 1) Scots-Irish, 2) English, or 3) German. As to the Scots-Irish theory, this is propounded by independent researcher Mrs. Betty Huber of Morrisville, a charter member of the Historic Morrisville Society, who has been studying the Hoops family for years. Although she has yet to identify Adam Hoops's birth place or ancestry, she believes
(continued...)

[8](...continued)
he was Scots-Irish, as he was one of the early settlers in that part of Lancaster County (later Cumberland County in 1750), which was heavily settled by immigrants from Ulster. (Ninety per cent of whom were Scots-Irish, according to Lester J. Cappon, ed., *Atlas of Early American History: Revolutionary Era, 1760-1790*, (Princeton, 1976), 98; James T. Lemon, *The Best Poor Man's Country: A Geographical Study of Early Southeastern Pennsylvania* (Baltimore, 1972), 50, fig. 13; and James G. Leyburn, *The Scotch-Irish: A Social History* (Chapel Hill, 1962), 198-99). This is a reasonable conclusion, as Hoops was a devout Presbyterian. The fact that Adam Hoops in 1763-64 spent several months in Ireland lends credence to this belief.

Supporting the English theory, Maria King wrote in her town history, *The History of Ceres and its Near Vicinity from its Early Settlement in 1798 to the Present* (Olean, N.Y., 1896), 25, that "Major Adam Hoops [youngest son of Adam Hoops]...had a genealogical record that went back to the 9th century. They were of English descent...." This information was repeated by Maud D. Brooks in *A Sketch of the Early Settlement Olean and its Founder Major Adam Hoops* (Olean, NY, 1898) with the additional comment that "Miss King...states that members of her family have seen this record" (28).

As to German origins, there is an intriguing entry in P. William Filby with Dorothy M. Lower, eds., *Passenger and Immigration Lists Index, 1991 Supplement* (Detroit, 1991) that an "Adam Hoop" emigrated from Liechtenstein to America at an unknown date. Checking the source of that statement—Norbert Jansen's *Nach Amerika! Geschichte der liechtensteinischen Auswanderung nach den Vereinigten Staaten von Amerika* (Vaduz, 1976), 188—we learned that this was a nineteenth-century immigration. Could Adam Hoops have been a German-speaking immigrant? His written English suggests his native language could well have been German. That does not explain his Presbyterianism, but perhaps he adopted his wife's religion. The architect and historian, Charles Morse Stotz, writes, without citing sources, that Hoops was German. "Defense in the Wilderness," *The Western Pennsylvania Historical Magazine*, 41 (autumn 1958, no. 3-4):97, and *Outposts of the War for Empire:The French and English in Western Pennsylvania: Their Armies, Their Forts, Their People, 1749-1764* (Pittsburgh, 1985), 27. The name Hoop, though rare, does appear throughout the Rhine valley—the eighteenth-century Palatinate—but no family of that name or any similar spelling appears in the lists of Palatine emigrants given by Walter A. Knittle, *Early Eighteenth Century Palatine Emigration: A British Government Redemptioner Project to Manufacture Naval Stores* (1937; Salem, Mass., 1999) or by I. Daniel Rupp, *A Collection of Upwards of Thirty Thousand Names of German, Swiss, Dutch, French, and Other Immigrants in Pennsylvania from 1727-1776: with a statement of the names of ships...also an appendix containing lists of more than one thousand German and French names in New York prior to 1712*. 2nd rev. and enl. Ed., (Philadelphia, 1898), microfiche.

The mystery may be solved if the missing "Hoops Bible" can be located. This Bible was described in an article in *The Christian-Evangelist* of November 8, 1900 written by Decima Campbell Barclay, wife of John Judson Barclay, great grandson of Thomas Barclay and great-great grandson of Adam Hoops. "I have now in my possession a much older Bible, which was published in London in 1696, during the reign of 'William and Mary'...This 'Family Bible' descended to my husband from his great grandmother, Mary Hoops, of Philadelphia, who was married to Thomas

(continued...)

on the western frontier of Pennsylvania in 1738.[9]   There is nothing to indicate he had much formal education; his handwriting was execrable and his spelling was, to put it kindly, distinctively phonetic. However, by sheer grit, hard work, and relentless drive he became one of Pennsylvania's first self-made men. Other Pennsylvanians were wealthier—Chief Justice William Allen, the Willings, the Shippens, the Cadwaladers, the Powels—but they inherited or married money or obtained it easily from their urban armchairs in their powdered wigs by their connections with the Penn family proprietors.[10]

---

[8](...continued)
Barclay in 1770, so that it must have been in the possession of the Hoops family many years prior to her birth." We thank George F. Miller of Historic Bethany, Bethany, West Virginia, for this reference.

One fact appears certain. Adam Hoops is not descended from the Quakers Joshua Hoopes and son Daniel of Chester County. Of Daniel's seventeen children none was named Adam. J. Smith Futhey and Gilbert Cope, *History of Chester County, Pennsylvania* (Philadelphia, 1881), 605-06.

[9] *History of Franklin County, Pennsylvania* (Chicago, 1887), 152; William Henry Egle, ed. *Notes and Queries Historical and Genealogical chiefly relating to Interior Pennsylvania* [Reprint Third Series], (Baltimore, 1970), 3:151.

[10] William Allen, 1704-1780, considered by most historians the wealthiest of them all, was also the best connected. He not only inherited from his father but was such a "faithful servant to the Penn family" that he controlled patronage for Pennsylvania for most of his life. Norman S. Cohen, "William Allen: Chief Justice of Pennsylvania, 1704-1780, " (PhD diss., Univ. of California, Berkeley, 1966), chap. 2; Edward F. DeLancey in "Chief Justice William Allen," *PMHB*, 1(1877):202-03; Ruth Moser Kistler, "William Allen, Founder of Allentown, Colonial Jurist, Industrialist and Loyalist," *Lehigh County Historical Society Proceedings*, 24 (1962):16-20; Carl and Jessica Bridenbaugh, *Rebels and Gentlemen: Philadelphia in the Age of Franklin,* 184-91; Gary B. Nash, "Slaves and Slaveowners in Colonial Philadelphia," *William and Mary Quarterly*, Third Series, 30, no.2 (April 1973): 250, and *The Urban Crucible: Social Change, Political Consciousness and the Origins of the American Revolution* (Cambridge, MA, 1979), 257; and Stephen Brobeck, "Changes in the Composition and Structure of Philadelphia Elite Groups, 1756-1790" (PhD diss., Univ. of Pennsylvania, 1973), 101-02.

The Shippen family wealth and their advantageous connections are covered in depth by Randolph Shipley Klein in his *Portrait of an Early American Family: The Shippens of Pennsylvania Across Five Generations* (Philadelphia, 1975).

For Thomas Willing's inherited wealth and family connections, see Thomas Willing Balch, *Willing Letters and Papers edited with a biographical essay of Thomas Willing of Philadelphia (1731-1821)* (Philadelphia, 1922), XLIV-XLV,120-122; Eugene R. Slaski, "Thomas Willing: Moderation During the American Revolution " (PhD diss., Florida State Univ., 1971), who calls him "probably the wealthiest man in Philadelphia in 1781," 278; and Thomas M. Doerflinger, *A Vigorous Spirit of Enterprise: Merchants and Economic Development in Revolutionary Philadelphia*,

(continued...)

Adam Hoops did not start off well-connected. He wore buckskin, carried a musket, had been a "whiskey kegg maker."[11] He had walked the Indian trails west of the Susquehanna selling his wares from wagons, trading with friendly Indians and fighting off bellicose ones. As an Indian trader, Hoops came to know the mountains, forests and paths of the Alleghenies. Living on his farm in the Conochocheague settlement near McDowell's Mill on the edge of Cumberland County in the 1750s, Hoops helped fortify log homes and organized frontier defense, riding out in the night with his neighbors to rescue settlers from burning cabins. Some of his own men had been killed by marauding Indians. He himself had been nearly scalped.[12]   As one of five road commissioners in 1755 Adam Hoops had spent a month supervising the cutting of a road from Shippensburg west to Raystown (today's Bedford), where none before existed.[13]   He knew

---

[10](...continued)

who writes that he was "arguably the bluest of Philadelphia's blue-blooded traders," 48.   The lavish life styles of the wealthy may be seen in George B. Tatum, *Philadelphia Georgian: the City House of Samuel Powel and some of its eighteenth-century neighbors* (Middletown, 1976) and Nicholas B. Wainwright, *Colonial Grandeur in Philadelphia, The House and Furniture of General John Cadwalader* (Philadelphia, 1964).

Special mention must be made of Thomas M. Doerflinger's *A Vigorous Spirit of Enterprise*, a masterful and perceptive study of the Philadelphia merchant community. Although Adam Hoops is not mentioned by name in Doerflinger's book—many of the tables and statistical data are of the 1770s-1790s, too late for Hoops— we recognize him throughout, as one of the "intense entrepreneurs who were tough, grasping, and willing to take large risks," (16), going it alone (19), not electing "to live in sumptuous town houses," (31) and being "psychologically prepared to move to a new city or undertake a new enterprise in order to advance their fortunes."(63).

[11] *Pennsylvania Archives* (hereafter PA), 1st ser., 2:14.

[12] Edward Shippen to his Wife, Mrs. Mary Shippen, Shippensburg 10th July 1755, "Some Shippen Letters, with Notes," *Historical Papers and Addresses of the Lancaster County Historical Society*, (1907; New York, Kraus Reprint, 1970), 11 (1906-1907): 5-7; Adam Hoops to James Burd, Canogogig July 9th 1755, Shippen Papers, vol. 1, p. 203, HSP; Adam Hoops to Gov. Morris, Cannogogig, Nov. 3d, 1755, PA, 1st ser., 2:462-63; Adam Hoops to Gov. Morris, Canegogig, Novr. the 6, 1755, ibid., 474-75; Charles Swaine to Governor Morris, July 8, 1755 in Howard N. Eavenson, *Map Maker & Indian Traders: an account of John Patten trader, arctic explorer, and map maker; Charles Swaine author, trader, public official, and arctic explorer; Theodorus Swaine Drage, clerk, trader, and Anglican priest* (Pittsburgh, 1949), 73-74, 181-82.

[13] John Armstrong, James Burd, William Buchanan, George Croghan and Adam
(continued...)

the Pennsylvania frontier as well as Philadelphia merchants knew their counting houses, their ledgers, and their ballrooms.

As far as we know, Hoops started with nothing, except a drive to succeed, financial shrewdness, extensive contact with the farmers and skilled artisans in Pennsylvania, and a good eye for fertile farm land. He hitched his wagon—literally and figuratively—to the British command in North America during those skirmishes for empire known to Americans as the French and Indian War. He made his fortune as a contractor of provisions to supply the British and provincial troops in western Pennsylvania in 1757-1760 [14] and with

---

[13](...continued)
Hoops were "nominated, authorized, and appointed" by Governor Robert Hunter Morris on 12 March 1755 "to reconnoitre, explore, and view the Country West and North of the Kittochtinny or Blue Hills, and of the Great Virginia Road leading from Harris' Ferry... 'with orders'...to survey and lay out such Roads as You shall judge more direct and commodious...," *Minutes of the Provincial Council of Pennsylvania*, (Harrisburg, 1851), 6:318-19. For more on this segment of Braddock's Road in Pennsylvania, see ibid. 6:320-21, 323-24. The five commissioners' report to Governor Morris dated April 16, 1755 is printed in ibid., 368-69, also in *Letters and Papers relating chiefly to the Provincial History of Pennsylvania with some notices of the writers* [by Thomas Balch], (Philadelphia, 1855), 36-39; and in [I. Daniel Rupp], *Early History of Western Pennsylvania and of the West, and of Western Expeditions and Campaigns from MDCCLIV to MDCCCXXXIII* , (Pittsburgh, 1846), 65-66. For an account of the expenses incurred in cutting this road, see William Henry Egle, ed., *Notes and Queries Historical and Genealogical chiefly relating to Interior Pennsylvania*, 12 vols., (1894-1896; Baltimore, 1970), 3rd ser., 2:135-37; also the following Adam Hoops's letters: to James Burd, March 17 and June 18, 1755, Burd-Shippen Papers, B B892p, American Philosophical Society (hereafter APS); to James Burd, Cannogogig July 29, 1755, Shippen Papers, vol.1, HSP, and "Adam Hoops cash advanced to laborers cutting the road" [1755], Burd-Shippen Papers, Miscellaneous, B B892p, APS.

[14] Hoops was "Agent to the Contractors for Victualling his Majesty's Forces," *Pennsylvania Journal*, December 11, 1760. During the Forbes campaign he was agent in the field for Joshua Howell, who in turn was Philadelphia agent for Baker, Kilby and Baker of London, who held the contract from the Treasury Board, London. (Lewis Namier, *England in the Age of the American Revolution*, 2nd ed., (London, 1963), 241-42; Stanley M. Pargellis, *Lord Loudoun in North America* (New Haven, 1933), 72-74; W. T. Baxter, *The House of Hancock: Business in Boston, 1724-1775* (Cambridge, MA., 1945), "Christopher Kilby and Government Contracts," 95-110, and chap. 9: "The French and Indian War, 1755-1763." In 1760 the victualling contract was given to Colebrooke, Colebrooke, Nesbitt and Franks of London, whose Philadelphia partners were William Plumsted and David Franks. "Contractors for supplying the Army with Provisions and Carriages," Donald H. Kent, Autumn L. Leonard, S. K. Stevens, John L. Tottenham and Louis M. Waddell, eds., *The Papers of Henry Bouquet*, 6 vols., (Harrisburg, 1951-1994), hereafter PHB, 4: 468-69; Ibid.,

(continued...)

this fortune financed Summerseat.

During his years in Cumberland County, Adam Hoops was not only a frontiersman, but also an active citizen. He had been elected the first coroner when that county was established in 1750 and had served on the first grand jury in Shippensburg. He was a landowner, a farmer, a trader, and also a businessman, supplying goods and credit to farmers and traders. Thus, Hoops was already a presence by the time General Edward Braddock came marching through western Pennsylvania in 1755 on his way to the Ohio.[15]

When Braddock and his troops needed supplies and transport and the colonies of Virginia and Maryland had promised him everything and produced next to nothing, Benjamin Franklin, that good Pennsylvanian and even better colonial, came to the rescue. Many of the wagons and horses he procured for General Braddock's laborious and ultimately ill-fated march to the Ohio were supplied by Adam Hoops. Working with William West and William Buchanan, Hoops also served as commissary to supply provisions for troops and defense west of the Susquehanna in 1756 and 1757.[16]

In 1758 General John Forbes was named to attempt again the capture of Fort Duquesne from the French. Learning from the logistical problems of General Braddock, Forbes knew that a reliable supply line was crucial to success. He therefore ordered "supply

---

[14](...continued)
6:562n1; Namier, op. cit., 242; Pennsylvania Journal, November 20, 1760.

British army contracts were very profitable for American merchants, though this subject has received little attention by historians, other than to note abuse and fraud. Governor Shirley of New York and some New York merchants were especially crafty at padding accounts. See Pargellis, Lord Loudoun in North America, 102-03; 135-41.

[15] Minutes of the Provincial Council of Pennsylvania , 5:467-68; PA, 2nd ser., 9:806; History of Cumberland and Adams Counties, Pennsylvania (Chicago, 1886), 131-32; Two Hundred Years in Cumberland County (Carlisle, 1951), photograph of "a court record at Shippensburg, 1750" showing [Adam] Hoops's name, 35; History of Franklin County, Pennsylvania (Chicago, 1887), 402; and Sewell Elias Slick, William Trent and the West (Harrisburg, 1947), 62.

[16] PA., 8th ser., 6:4865-4866, 4875,4879, 4884; ibid., 1st ser., 2:601,603; ibid., 5th ser., 1:31, 44; ibid., 6th ser., 11:153-54; Lewis Burd Walker, ed., The Settlement of the Waggoners' Accounts Relating to General Braddock's Expedition towards Fort Du Quesne by Edward Shippen, et al., commissioners [from the Burd Shippen Papers](Philadelphia, 1899), 72-74; W. W. Abbott et al, eds., The Papers of George Washington, Colonial Ser., 6 vols. (Charlottesville, 1983), 2:151-52 n3; Minutes of the Provincial Council of Pennsylvania, 7:242; Leonard W. Labaree et al, eds. The Papers of Benjamin Franklin, (New Haven, 1963), 6:396,439; 7:4.

deposits" to be erected along the route from Carlisle to Fort Duquesne. Long before Napoleon, Forbes, the intrepid Scot, knew that his army marched on its stomach.

The staff officer in charge of keeping those stomachs filled and the supply wagons coming was the Swiss-born Colonel Henry Bouquet, General Forbes's second in command. Methodical, detail-oriented, well-organized and popular with the colonists, Colonel Bouquet—to Pennsylvanians the real hero of the French and Indian War—drew up a comprehensive "Detail of a Proposed Expedition to Fort DuQuesne." Bouquet's estimate for one month's provisions for 2160 men was: 300 oxen, 100 barrels of pork, 100,000 pounds of flour, 45 hogsheads of rum, 4000 lbs. of tobacco, 10,000 pounds of rice, 8000 lbs. of butter in casks, and 8000 lbs. of cheese.[17]

When the expedition finally got under way in May 1758, it involved over six thousand troops, wagoners, and road cutters. From Carlisle they marched, slid, stumbled, waded, and plodded 200 miles west through dense forests, over inhospitable mountains, and across swollen streams. Six months it would take to reach the Ohio and dislodge the French. It would also take 546 tons of beef, over 300 tons of pork, 624 tons of flour, 39 tons of rice, 58,500 pounds of butter, hundreds of hogsheads of rum and whiskey, more than three hundred wagons, and over 2000 horses. Adam Hoops supplied much of this.[18]

---

[17] "Bouquet: Expenses of Proposed Expedition Against Fort Duquesne [Philadelphia, March 18, 1757]," PHB, 1:55. Bouquet drafted this in March 1757 for Lord Loudoun, commander in chief of American forces. Loudoun, however, was relieved in December 1757 and replaced by Major-General James Abercromby, at which time John Forbes was promoted to brigadier general in America and named to head the expedition to Fort Duquesne.

[18] These figures are estimates based on the weekly allowance of rations per person fixed by Lord Loudoun and followed by his successors in America during the 1758-1759 campaign. These rations were 7 lbs. bread or the same amount of flour, 7 lbs. of beef or 4 lb. pork, 3 pints of peas, 1 lb. of cheese or 6 oz. butter, and 1 lb. flour or 1/2 lb. rice. PHB, 1:89,142; Alfred Procter James, ed., *Writings of General John Forbes Relating to his Service in North America*, (Menasha, WI, 1938), 122. Contracts between Adam Hoops and General Forbes and Colonel Bouquet have not been found. General Forbes wrote Colonel Bouquet on July 14, 1758, enclosing "Mr Hoops Calculation of provisions by which you will see that wee have 3 months provision for Six thousand men at Raes Town...," but that enclosure has not been found. Ibid., 145-147; PHB, 2:207-08. The Return of Provisions sent in periodically to General Forbes from the different posts gives an idea of quantities supplied by Adam Hoops: "A Return of Provisions in Store belonging to the Contractors at the Sundry Posts & Forts on the Route towards fort Duquesne with a Calculation how

(continued...)

The feats of organization and manpower needed in western Pennsylvania to transport these provisions, to drive the cattle and hogs, and to walk the heavily laden horse-drawn wagons defy today's comprehension. There were no highways, no bridges, no trucks, no refrigeration. There was not even a road. That was being cut in advance of the marching regiments through the "immense Forest of 240 Miles of Extent, intersected by several ranges of Mountas [sic] - impenetrable almost to any thing humane...."[19] "Raftts and flatts" were hewn on the spot to cross the rivers, sometimes swollen with rains.[20]   Wagons sank in the mud, wheels broke, horses drowned, men got drunk, bags split, rain washed out the road and flour spoiled. There were mosquitoes, fleas, rats, extreme cold, and stifling heat. Yet they all marched on.

Barrels, bags, and baskets were the packaging, horses and

---

[18](...continued)
long it will serve 6000 Men Aug 23 1758," Dalhousie Muniments, *Papers Relating to America in the Dalhousie Muniments* (hereafter *Dalhousie Muniments*), Scottish Record Office, General Register, Edinburgh, Microfilm reel II.GD.45/2/2-105 (Papers and Correspondence Relating to John Forbes), II.GD.45/2/37/5; "Return of Provisions at Raystown November 13, 1758" by Daniel Clark, *Dalhousie Muniments*, II.GD.45/2/90/15; "A State of the Provisions at and abt Lancaster and Carlisle belonging to the Contractors Decr 15 1758," listing 50,000 lbs. of flour, 950 barrels of flour, 100 barrels of pork, & 25,000 lbs. of beef, Daniel Clark to John St. Clair, Deputy Quartermaster General, PHB, 2:630; "By a letter from Hoops the following Provisions at Lancaster, Carlisle, Fort Loudoun, & Fort Littleton, is ready to be sent up whenever their are Carriages or Horses provided: 1075 Barrils, 38 Baggs, 40,000 lbs. bulk flour, 182 Barrils of Pork, 4 Barrils of Beef, 25,000 Pounds of Beef at Carlisle, 18 Barrils of Rice, Hoggs upon the Road from Winchester to the amount of 50,000 lb." Halket to Bouquet, 29th December 1758, PHB, 2:648-49; "A Return of Provisions at Pittsburgh the 1st of January 1759" unsigned, *Dalhousie Muniments*, II.GD.45/2/37/7; "A Return of the Number of Waggons, left at the Following Places, Between Pittsburg & Carlisle" undated, George Morton, Superintendent of Waggons, *Dalhousie Muniments*, II.GD.45/2/37/8.

[19] General John Forbes to William Pitt, Carlisle, 10 July 1758, *Dalhousie Muniments*, II.GD.45/2/52/1a. The distances from camp to camp and landmark to landmark between Carlisle and Pittsburgh varied with the person doing the measuring. Estimates ranged from 193 to 213 miles. See "Road Reports of Baker, Clayton, and Ward," PHB, 2:234, 236, 237 and "Distance from Pittsburgh to Carlisle, c. December, 1758," ibid., 2:651-52. Compare with Archer Butler Hulbert, *The Old Glade (Forbes') Road (Pennsylvania State Road)*, Historic Highways of America, 16 vols., (Cleveland, 1903), 5:121-22.

[20] "The Susquehanna is so much swelled by the latest rains that it took nearly three days to ferry thirty wagons across..." Bouquet to Forbes, May 25, 1758, PHB, 1:357, 361.

wagons were the transport, and salt was used to keep the meat from spoiling. Wagons—and the lack of them—had been the bugbear of every British commander since General Braddock arrived in Virginia in 1755 to find none. Locating hundreds of wagons and persuading the Americans to lend them—at a price, of course—was a never-ending search. "The Waggons have been the plague of my life," Forbes grumbled to Bouquet.[21] So when Adam Hoops managed to come up with 180 wagons during a recruiting trip, when Colonel Bouquet could locate only eight, it is no surprise that Bouquet was "well satisfied" with Hoops.[22]

Time and again Hoops showed his organizational talents, his wide range of contacts and his "indefatigability." For Forbes and Bouquet he was all over the map, which in 1758 included the then eight counties of Pennsylvania, the Lower Three (now Delaware), northern Maryland and western Virginia. He crisscrossed Cumberland, Lancaster and York counties for horses and wagons,[23] he contracted with a miller in York County for flour,[24] he visited a storekeeper near Dunkard's Creek (western Virginia) to inspect 200 barrels of pork,[25] he arranged to have piles of "provender for horses along the route to Raes Town (Bedford),"[26] and he rode off to Fort

---

[21] *Writings of General John Forbes*, 146; PHB, 2:207. And it was not just any old wooden wagon that would do. Each had to have "four good strong Horses, properly harnessed...; it was to be 'large and strong..., having a Drag Chain, eleven Feet in Length, with a Hook at each End, a Knife for cutting Grass, Falling-Axe, and Shovel, two Setts of Clouts, and five Setts of Nails, and Iron Hoop to the End of every Axletree, a Linen Mangoe, a two Gallon Kegg of Tar and Oil mixed together; a Slip, Bell, Hopples, two Setts of Shoes, and four Setts of Shoe Nails for each Horse; two Setts of spare Hames, and five Setts of Hame-strings; a Bag to receive their Provisions; a spare Sett of Linch Pins, and a Hand Screw for every Six Waggons....'" "Forbes Advertisement for Wagons, Horses, Drivers, etc. in *Pennsylvania Gazette*, May 11, 1758," cited in the *Writings of General John Forbes*, 88-89.

[22] " ...After all the efforts I have made for four days, I have been able to obtain only eight wagons up to the present time...I just now received a letter from Mr. Hoops which informs me that he hopes very easily to obtain the 180 wagons I have asked from the three counties...This man is very energetic, and I am well satisfied with him...." Bouquet to Forbes, May 29 & 30, 1758, PHB, 1:386-90.

[23] Ibid. 2:105-06.

[24] George Stevenson to Thomas Donnellan, May 25, 1758, Ibid., 1:371.

[25] PHB, 2:47-48, 51, 57.

[26] Ibid. 2:135.

Cumberland in Maryland to meet the convoy coming from Virginia.[27]

When he was not out making the rounds of the forts or cajoling farmers to lend their better horses, Hoops worked out of Carlisle, where he was then living. There he supervised a staff of clerks, managed a network of agents at every fort,[28] entered into a partnership with Dr. Thomas Walker to provide "for the subsistence of" Virginia troops,[29] established a courier service ("Hoops's express"),[30] sent off assistants to Fort Cumberland in Maryland to find wagons "to Bring up the N: Carolina Troops & Some Barreled Beef from Alexandria,"[31] oversaw the weighing and bagging of oats, flour, and rice, and organized the loading of wagons as they were brought into Carlisle, sending rice and butter to Fort Loudoun "for the use of the sick," pork to Shippensburg, and flour, salt and wagon cloths to Fort Bedford.[32]

There were times, though, when even Adam Hoops despaired. Colonel Bouquet advised General Forbes not to complain, "... I think that if we object to his flour, he will give up the undertaking, which would be worse, under the circumstances, than grey flour; for such an industrious man, and one so well acquainted with the country, could not easily be found...."[33]

Now approaching age fifty, Hoops continued "to run night and day." [34] He spent days in the saddle; in one case he covered the more than one hundred miles between Philadelphia and Carlisle in two days.[35] As the campaign advanced, he was asked to take on more and more responsibility. He transported on horseback £10,000

[27] Ibid., 393-94, 397-98.

[28] For reference to two such employees, see the *Dictionary of Canadian Biography*, 13 vols. to date (Toronto, 1966-), 6: 30-31, "Charles Baker," and Walter T. Kamprad, "John Ormsby, Pittsburgh's Original Citizen," *Western Pennsylvania Historical Magazine*, 23 (1940): 203-22.

[29] PHB, 2: 84,87.

[30] Ibid., 413; *Writings of General Forbes*, 210.

[31] PHB, 2:133.

[32] Ibid., 129.

[33] Bouquet to Forbes, Carlisle, June 7, 1758, PHB, 2:43, 48.

[34] Ibid., 95,97.

[35] "Your favr of the 15th Inst I reced on my Return from Philadelphia which I Compleated in two Days..." Hoops to Bouquet, Carlisle, June 17, 1758, Ibid., 105-06.

sterling from General Forbes in Philadelphia to the paymaster in Lancaster.[36] He helped plan and supervise the layout and construction of the storehouses at Fort Bedford. He advised on the building of smoke houses at Fort Ligonier. He oversaw the slaughter of 1500 cattle. He organized the storehouses in Carlisle and arranged holding pens for the hundreds of cattle, sheep and hogs until they could be driven to the "upper forts."[37] It was to Adam Hoops that Colonel Bouquet turned when the Virginians supplied unacceptably lean and scrawny cattle.[38]

Adam Hoops's methods alienated some people, raised questions from others, and provoked complaints. General Forbes questioned Hoops's penny-pinching.[39] The young colonel George Washington was displeased because Hoops's assistant at Fort Cumberland refused to provide salt for the fresh meat.[40] A Virginia captain complained of his withholding provisions,[41] York County officials complained of his rudeness and his overbearing tactics,[42] and Colonel Armstrong

---

[36] Ibid. 1:345; 350-51.

[37] Ibid., 350-51; 2:211, 393-94, 397-98, 628-29.

[38] "We received 300 [cattle] yesterday from Virginia, small, lean and as poor as they could be. I have forbidden Hoops to take a single one more from that province, and to buy what he will need for salting in Pennsylvania where there are some in abundance all the time..." Bouquet to Forbes, Rays Town Camp, August 26, 1758, Ibid., 2:422, 424.

[39] "Mr Killby's Deputes Mr Howell and Mr Hoops may be extream good people in their way, and very proper for providing a Garrison of 100 men, but their Ideas & ways of judging of things are so narrow and Contracted, that all my Rhetorick Cannot drive it into their Heads that it is better for me to have a months provisions over, as that the Army should run a risque of being stopt for the want of one days Subsisting." Forbes to Abercromby, August 11, 1758, *Writings of General Forbes*, 172-75. And "Mr. Hoops is a good man but his Ideas and Compass of Genius for the subsistence and maintainance of the Army are all triffling and narrow, eternally Bothering upon the saving of sixpences & two pences, so must be managed accordingly." Forbes to Bouquet, August 18, 1758, PHB, 2:382-84.

[40] "...A dispute has arose between an Assistant Commissary of Mr Hoops (namely Mr Joseph Gailbraith) and I, abt Salt-Our Stock of Meat is mostly Fresh and he refuses to provide Salt for it..." George Washington to Henry Bouquet, 3rd July 1758, W. W. Abbott, ed., *The Papers of George Washington*, 5:260; PHB, 2:159-60.

[41] W. W. Abbott, ed., *The Papers of George Washington*, 6:184-85.

[42] "As you have an aversion to 'long' Letters which you cant answer, we must be Brief to please You. Your Letter to Mr. Lesher has in it such Reflections on the Magistrates of this County as his Excellcy General Forbes would despise you for. You are no

(continued...)

groused about Hoops's profits.[43] Hoops ran a tight organization. He ruffled feathers and made enemies. He was undoubtedly not an easy man to deal with and did not take criticism lightly, but he produced results.[44]   His word and deed were as good as his spelling and grammar were bad. Colonel Bouquet knew his man and not only stood by him, but, as we shall see below, he also called upon him for his own personal services.

When Fort Duquesne finally fell to the English without a shot in November 1758—the French burned it and fled—it became Fort Pitt (and later Pittsburgh) with an English garrison. Hoops continued supplying Fort Pitt with meat and flour and rounded up wagons during 1759 and 1760. But he let the major contract lapse, when he decided to move east.[45]

With the French driven out of western Pennsylvania and the back country no longer disturbed by marauding Indian tribes, England reduced the number of troops stationed in the provinces, appointed General Robert Monckton as commander in chief of southern forces, and switched its battle operations from the colonies to the Caribbean.

---

[42](...continued)
Officer in the Army unless your employment under a very worthy Gentleman Mr. Joshua Howell (who is against bearing Arms) constitutes you such. You have much Impudence but have not Courage enough in person to behave to Magistrates whom you charged with 'barefaced Excuses' with the same Rudeness you have treated us with in the Above Letter to Mr. Lesher." Letter to Adam Hoops from Willm Bird, Wm Maugridge, Jonas Seiby, Peter Spycker, James Read, Reading, October 3, 1758. *Dalhousie Muniments*, II.GD.45/2/2/90/11.

[43] "The Contract with Messrs. Hoops & Buchanan gives a general Umbrage, and was the most mistaken thing I ever knew...the Service is like to be retarded, and nothing saved to the Publick, but an Extravagant sum thrown into the hands of two private persons for a Service of not more than two months in ye whole year." Col. Armstrong to [Edward Shippen ? Gov. Denny is mistakenly named as the addressee], Carlisle November 11, 1756, PA, 1st ser., 3:48-49. See also Leonard W. Labaree, ed., *The Papers of Benjamin Franklin*, 7:102 n1.

[44] "I Make no Doubt but I may be Sometimes Deficient in my Duty which I Cannot help as the Troops are so Scattered and So Much to Do...But that Method which Collo Stephens has Introduced I am Resolved not to put up with...," Adam Hoops to Bouquet, June 9, 1758, PHB, 2:59. "By a letter from Hoops I see that he has sent me everything I needed..." Bouquet to Forbes, June 22, 1758, Ibid., 125-26; 126-27.

[45] "On the 25th day of March next the Contractors delivers [sic] over all these Provisions on hand, at all the different Posts, and Garrisons, to such persons as will be appointed to receive them, and those is not known yet...." Adam Hoops to Thomas Walker, January 17, 1760, Thomas Walker Papers in the William Cabell Rives Papers, Reel 2, container 162, LC.

General Monckton came to Pennsylvania in 1760, visited the western forts, and stayed a while in Philadelphia, where he made the acquaintance of Adam Hoops, before sailing off to attack Martinique. Hoops and Monckton would become close friends.[46]

Hoops was by now more than a source of supplies to the British commanders. He was agent and financial advisor for Colonel Bouquet, helping him find a millwright for his Maryland farm, and lending him money.[47] Colonel Frederick Haldimand, another Swiss in America during the French and Indian War, and later General and Commander of forces in Quebec and West Florida, called on Hoops to manage his property in Bedford County, to have it surveyed, to find tenants and to collect the rents.[48]

In May 1761 Adam Hoops packed up his family—five daughters, one son-in-law and three sons—and moved to Third Street in Philadelphia, property he had purchased in 1759.[49] However, he never

---

[46] "In my last I had the pleasure of acknowledging your Excellencies much Esteem'd present...The great willingness that you have always shewed to Oblige, and the many favours I have recd at your Hands have encouraged me once more to bespeak your Excellencies Friendship and Assistance." Adam Hoops to General Monckton, Philadelphia February 22, 1769, The Aspinwall Papers, *Collections of the Massachusetts Historical Society* (Boston, 1871), 4th ser., 10:604-08.

[47] PHB, 4:589; 5:157, 237-38, 380-81, 434; Adam Hoops to Colonel Bouquet, Philadelphia, March 3, 1762, *The Papers of Colonel Henry Bouquet*, Series 21648, Part 1, mimeog. ed. (Harrisburg, 1942), 41; Adam Hoops to Colonel Bouquet, Philadelphia, November 12, 1762, *The Papers of Colonel Henry Bouquet*, Part 2, 148. In Henry Bouquet's will dated April 19, 1765, he left instructions to pay a debt of "Five hundred & fifty Pounds Currency" to Adam Hoops. The Papers of Henry Bouquet, Additional MSS 21660, p. 23138, photostats at LC.

[48] Adam Hoops to General Haldimand, December 9, 1766, February 5 and May 1, 1767, Haldimand Papers, British Museum Additional MSS 21728, Pt. 3, photostats at LC; Adam Hoops to General Haldimand, August 23, 1767, Haldimand Papers, Pt. 4; Adam Hoops to General Haldimand, February 11, 1768, Haldimand Papers, Pt. 5; Adam Hoops to General Haldimand, June 10, 1768, Haldimand Papers, Pt. 7.

[49] Two houses were on the property purchased from William Henderson, but we do not know which one the Hoops family occupied. Located next to each other on the east side of Third between Mulberry and Sassafras Streets (today's Arch and Race Streets), both were three stories, with separate kitchens. Given Hoops's large family, he probably selected the southernmost house, which was the larger of the two—17 1/2 ft. by 39 1/2 ft.—and had "a marble chimney piece in the back & front Parlours." In 1756 this was the house "where Lynford Lardner dwells." Deed of Indenture between William Henderson and Adam Hoops dated June 2, 1759, Deed Book H-10, pp. 43-47, Philadelphia City Hall, Recorder of Deeds. Policy Nos. 357 and 358 for the William Henderson houses, surveyed by Joseph Fox, December 7,

(continued...)

severed his ties with Carlisle and Cumberland County. He leased his large stone house in the main square, remained active in promoting the Presbyterian Church there, served as administrator for the Orphans' Court, and continued to buy up good farm land in that county.[50]

Settled in the thriving commercial center that was Philadelphia, the largest city in the colonies in the 1760s, Adam Hoops expanded his portfolio and diversified his financial investments. He bought land, property, warehouses, estates, ships, and an iron furnace. He was quick to take advantage of economic opportunity and was an industrialist before his time.

He was also a one-man financial institution in a time when there were no banks, no checks, no savings and loans, no stock market. Those with cash on hand, one of whom was obviously Adam Hoops, weathered the downturn in the economy which followed the end of the War and the signing of the treaty of 1763. Those less fortunate, or provident, borrowed from Hoops. The number of persons to whom he lent money grew larger, including a future President of the United States, the young James Madison.[51]

---

[49](...continued)
1756, transfer to Adam Hoops recorded March 25, 1768, The Philadelphia Contributionship Companies. We are greatly indebted to Carol Wojtowicz Smith for the above information and for copies of these policies.

[50] Concerning this house in Carlisle, "the model for excellence for the stone masons," see Allan D. Thompson, *The Meeting House on the Square: an Historical Sketch of the First Presbyterian Church of Carlisle, Pennsylvania* (Carlisle, 1964), 31; *Two Hundred Years in Cumberland County*, 47; Merrilou Scribner Schaumann, *A History and Genealogy of Carlisle, Cumberland County, Pennsylvania, 1751-1835* (Carlisle, 1995), Lot #173 (9-15 N. Hanover Street), 95-96; Allen Weinberg and Thomas E. Slattery, comps., *Warrants and Surveys of the Province of Pennsylvania including the Three Lower Counties. 1759* (Philadelphia, 1965), 27. Copies of the surveys by Nicholas Scull are in the Cumberland County Historical Association and Hamilton Library, Warrant & Survey for Lot 173, Flat MS. 2-10. Hoops's house was being used by British officers—leased by Colonel Bouquet?—in 1764. *Bouquet's March to the Ohio*, 52 53.

Hoops was one of the trustees of the Presbyterian Church in Carlisle, being named in the deed from Thomas and Richard Penn, dated September 20, 1766, granting a lot of ground for a church. Allan D. Thompson, *The Meeting House on the Square*, 30-31. He also sold lottery tickets to raise funds to build a Presbyterian Church in Carlisle, *Pennsylvania Gazette*, June 24 & July 2, 1762. For reference to Hoops's administering a sale for the Orphans Court, see the *Pennsylvania Journal*, March 28, 1765.

[51] William T. Hutchinson and William M. E. Rachal, eds., *The Papers of James*
(continued...)

In March 1761, when Colonel Bouquet wrote General Monckton from Fort Pitt, "We are in great want of shoes, none to be had at this Place," Hoops arranged for a tanner and shoemaker to set up business there, lending the capital and the hides.[52] He provided seed money for son-in-law Daniel Clark and was the silent partner in his mercantile business, a business cited by many historians who have studied the informative Clark Letterbook in the Historical Society of Pennsylvania.[53] Judging from documented cases we have seen of Hoops providing financial support to Clark, bailing him out, for instance, when he failed, we suspect that he also helped him buy a

---

[51](...continued)
Madison, 17 vols. (Chicago and Charlottesville, 1962-1991), 1:48-50.

Part of the estate papers attached to Adam Hoops's will is a list of sixty persons, identified by initials only, indebted to him for mortgages, bonds, rents, notes, and interest. These assets totaled £25,000. Will no. 79, 1771, Office of the Recorder of Wills, Philadelphia City Hall. For other references to Hoops as creditor, see Schaumann, *A History and Genealogy of Carlisle, Cumberland County, Pennsylvania, 1751-1835*, 89; PA, 8th ser., 8:6754-6755; and the Bond between William Long and James Watson and the Executors of the Estate of Adam Hoops, dated May 8, 1782, Cumberland County Historical Association and Hamilton Library, 29-5.

[52] Bouquet to Monckton, Fort Pitt, March 18, 1761, The Aspinwall Papers, *Collections of the Massachusetts Historical Society*, 4th ser., 9:392-93; Adam Hoops to Colonel Bouquet, April 21, 1761, PHB, 5:434.

[53] "Daniel Clark, Having moved from his House, on the South Side of Market-Street, to the House where Mr. Alexander M'Gee lately lived, has to sell, for Cash or short Credit, at the Store lately occupied by Messieurs Standley and Fullton, a Neat Assortment of dry Goods, which he imported in the last Vessels from London and Liverpool." *Pennsylvania Gazette*, July 2, 1761, *Pennsylvania Journal*, July 30, 1761; *Pennsylvania Gazette*, December 10, 1761 and July 22, 1762; *Pennsylvania Journal*, July 29, 1762; Daniel Clark Letterbook, 1759-1761, HSP. Some of the scholars who have trolled this collection and have cited Clark's very quotable letters are: Anne Bezanson, Robert D. Gray, and Miriam Hussey, *Prices in Colonial Pennsylvania* (Philadelphia, 1935), 39-40, 69, 109, 127, 140, 175-76, 203, 278-79, 432; Arthur L. Jensen, *The Maritime Commerce of Colonial Philadelphia*, 2nd pr. (Madison, 1966), 79-80, 86, 119-120, 251n, 254n, 262n, 265n, 299; Harry D. Berg, "The Organization of Business in Colonial Philadelphia, *Pennsylvania History*, 10 (July 1943, no. 3):167-68, and "Economic Consequences of the French and Indian War for the Philadelphia Merchants," *Pennsylvania History*, 13 (1946):186-91; John J. McCusker, *Money and Exchange in Europe and America, 1600-1775: A Handbook* (Chapel Hill, 1977), 188; Thomas Doerflinger, *A Vigorous Spirit of Enterprise*, 104, 370-71, Table A-4; Sharon V. Salinger, *"To serve well and faithfully": Labor and Indentured Servants in Pennsylvania, 1682-1800* (New York, 1987), 75; and Harrold E. Gillingham, "Lotteries in Philadelphia Prior to 1776," *Pennsylvania History*, 5 (January-October 1938):90.

share in the ship *Jenny* and helped him underwrite marine insurance policies for the years 1762-1770.[54]

In Philadelphia Hoops bought stores and lots on Market and Front Streets, wharves on the waterfront,[55] and the property on Third Street known later as the Byrd-Penn-Chew house.[56]

---

[54] Clark was one of three owners of the *Jenny*, a 90-ton, Philadelphia-built ship, registered December 8, 1762. (Records of the Port of Philadelphia, 1727-1804. Declarations of British Registry of Vessels, 1727-1776, Roll 3, frame 627, Pennsylvania Historical and Museum Commission (hereafter PHMC), Harrisburg. Microfilm copy; *Pennsylvania Journal*, October 27, 1763). He also was one of three owners of the brigantine *Sally*, registered February 18, 1761. "Ship Registers for the Port of Philadelphia, 1726-1775," PMHB, 27:106. As a marine underwriter, see Harrold E. Gillingham, *Marine Insurance in Philadelphia, 1721-1800* (Philadelphia, 1933), 56.

In April 1769 Adam Hoops deeded some property in Carlisle "for love and affection and 5 shillings to his son-in-law Daniel Clark, gentleman of Philadelphia" to help him pay off his debts. A month later the Clarks sold these two lots to his creditors Jeremiah Warder, Abel James and William West of Philadelphia. Merri Lou Scribner Schaumann, *A History and Genealogy of Carlisle, Cumberland County, Pennsylvania, 1751-1835*, 148-49. He also deeded some of his Cumberland County farm land to Clark to help him pay off debts. PA, 3rd ser., 2:45-46. In his will dated June 7, 1771, Adam Hoops bequeathed to his daughter Jane Clark "one thousand pounds (which I paid to her said husband more than a year ago)." He also stated that "whatever Daniel Clark had of me before he failed shall not be accounted to him I having received by dividend of the proceeds of his effects." Will no.79, 1771, Office of the Recorder of Wills, Philadelphia City Hall.

[55] Deed of Indenture between John Malcolm sailmaker and wife Margaret and Adam Hoops dated December 27, 1760 for house and lot on Front Street, Deed Book H-15, 124-28; Deed of Indenture between Grace Caldwell, John Mease, William Allison and Samuel Caldwell, executors for estate of David Caldwell, and Adam Hoops, dated 16 March 1763 for house and lot on Front Street, Deed Book H-17, 423-27; Deed of Indenture between Thomas Bourne and wife Margaret and Adam Hoops dated February 18, 1761 for "a certain messuage or tenement and piece of ground on the river Delaware..." (docks), Deed Book H-14, 13-16, Philadelphia Recorder of Deeds.

The Hoops docks, at the end of High or Market Street, are shown on the 1762 map of Philadelphia, reproduced as the Clarkson-Biddle Map in Martin P. Snyder, *City of Independence: Views of Philadelphia Before 1800* (New York, 1975), fig. 27, and on the same map labeled "Philadelphia c.1760 after Nicholas Scull, Plan of the improved part of the City [of Philadelphia] (1762)" in the *Atlas of Early American History*, 10.

[56] Deed of Indenture between William Byrd and wife Mary and Adam Hoops, dated November 27, 1764, Deed Book I-7, 278-80 and Deed of Indenture between Adam Hoops and wife Elizabeth and William Allen, dated February 4, 1765, Deed Book I-7, 281-83. Philadelphia Recorder of Deeds. George R. Tatum, *Philadelphia Georgian: the City House of Samuel Powel and Some of Its Eighteenth-century Neighbors*, 145

(continued...)

His ships traded to London, Liverpool, Amsterdam, Cadiz, Lisbon, Newry, Belfast, Barcelona, and the Bay of Fundy.[57]   His investment of a one-sixth share in the privateer *Hawke* was less successful, although he did not lose money.   In July 1762 this schooner, "mounting fourteen carriage and sixteen swivel guns, carrying eighty men" set out with much fanfare "on a Cruize against His Majesty's Enemies."[58]   Two weeks after launching, she capsized

---

[56](...continued)
n16.

[57] Hoops's ships were the snow *Elizabeth*, trading to Newry, Liverpool, Amsterdam, Lisbon and Barcelona ("Ship Registers for the Port of Philadelphia, 1726-1775," PMHB, 27:347; *Pennsylvania Gazette*, October 22, November 5 and 26, 1761; July 1 and 22 and November 25, 1762; *Pennsylvania Journal*, October 22 and November 26, 1761; September 22, 1763; July 12 and August 2, 1764; May 1, 1766); the ship *Polly* ("Ship Registers for the Port of Philadelphia, 1726-1775," PMHB, 27:106; *Pennsylvania Journal*, October 1 and 22, November 26, 1761; *Pennsylvania Gazette*, October 22, November 5 and 26, 1761; September 9 and 16, 1762), trading to Sligo, Liverpool, and Holland in 1764, bringing in several hundred German emigrants (*Pennsylvania Journal*, Sept 20, 1764); the schooner *Jane*, formerly the *Dolly*, built in Salisbury, Massachusetts in 1760 and bought by Hoops in 1762 (Records of the Port of Philadelphia, 1727-1804. Record Group 41. Declarations of British Registry of Vessels, 1727-1776, vol. I. Microfilm Roll 3, frame 594, PHMC); ship *New Hope*, on which he and his family sailed to Europe in June 1763, later trading to New York, London, Bristol, Liverpool, Cork, Belfast, Halifax, Lisbon, and Cadiz (Records of the Port of Philadelphia, 1727-1804. Record Group 41. Declarations of British Registry of Vessels, 1727-1776, vol. 1. Microfilm Roll 3, frame 651, PHMC; *Pennsylvania Journal*, June 2 and 16, July 7, 1763; February 23, March 29, April 12 and 26; September 13; November 1 and 15, 1764; May 1, 1766). Hoops may also have had a share in the Schooner *Rose* (along with the Wallaces of New York), trading to the Bay of Fundy to supply the Hopewell township in Nova Scotia (*Pennsylvania Journal*, August 7, 1766). In addition, Hoops had shares in two privateers.

[58] "...Am obliged to you for your good wishes to our Privater, she will be Lanched in in [sic] two weeks & I hope a full match for any of French or Spanish frigates indeed she is the finest ship ever was built in North America I hold the 5 of her as yet...I have 6 part of the privateer Hake [*Hawke*] of 14 Guns which sailed about two Weeks agoe, & I have 3 Ships in the Merchant trade which is enough for me to venture at sea...." Adam Hoops to Colonel Bouquet, June 8, 1762, *The Papers of Colonel Henry Bouquet*, Series 21648, Pt. 1, 138. Mimeog. ed. *Pennsylvania Gazette*, April 29 and May 20, 1762.
     We have not been able to identify the second privateer mentioned by Hoops in his letter to Colonel Bouquet, although it was probably the one alluded to in the *Pennsylvania Journal* of May 6, 1762: "We have now building a fine ship of 94 Feet Keel, for a Privateer to be commanded by Capt. Appowen." Hoops evidently was pleased with his share in this venture, as he had also mentioned it in two earlier letters to Colonel Bouquet, May 4, 1762 and in a missing letter of April (?), 1762. *The*
                                                                (continued...)

off the coast of Providence and sank with a loss of twenty-five of her crew.[59]

Adam Hoops's investments extended beyond Philadelphia. In 1765 he purchased 1,250 acres in Sussex County, New Jersey. This estate, later known by the name of Belvidere, was managed by Adam's son, Robert, who became a prominent and active citizen of Sussex County.[60] Hoops settled his daughter and son-in-law Jane and Daniel Clark on an estate in Lower Makefield Township in Bucks County which he bought at a sheriff's sale in 1770.[61] He owned

---

[58](...continued)
Papers of Colonel Henry Bouquet, Series 21648, Pt. 1, 96.

[59] *Pennsylvania Gazette*, August 19, 1762; Harrold E. Gillingham, *Marine Insurance in Philadelphia, 1721-1800*, 71. Hoops had insured his share for £500. He also was an underwriter of marine insurance policies, perhaps in conjunction with his son-in-law, with the Kidd and Bradford office in Philadelphia during the years 1762-1770. Ibid., 57.

[60] Indenture between Thomas and Richard Penn and Adam Hoops, October 2, 1765, Miscellaneous Manuscripts Collection, APS Library. This property had originally been purchased by Robert Patterson, who defaulted on his mortgage. Adam Hoops's ownership was evidently unknown to James P. Snell et al, compilers of the *History of Sussex and Warren Counties, New Jersey*, (Philadelphia, 1881), 32, 532-34. This "plantation in West Jersey called Paquess" was bequeathed in Hoops's will to his son Robert "together with the grist mill and two saw mills...store and store goods which he has now in his possession." (Will no.79, 1771, Office of the Recorder of Wills, Philadelphia City Hall). The Marquis de Chastellux describes a visit to Belvidere in 1782 in his *Travels in North America in the Years 1780, 1781 and 1782*, trans. and ed. Howard C. Rice, Jr. (Chapel Hill, 1963), 2: 518-21, where he garbles the name of Mrs. Robert Hoops's family. The name was Cottnam, not "Scotland." Robert's wife, Martha and her lawyer brother, George, were children of Arthur Cottnam, prominent Trenton attorney. Robert Hoops put the estate up for sale in February 1791, at which time it was advertised as having "500 acres with grist and saw mills, a store for dry goods, distillery, ferry house and shad fishery." *Brunswick Gazette*, February 22, 1791 as cited in *Notices from New Jersey Newspapers, 1781-1790*, *Records of New Jersey*, vol. 1, by Thomas B. Wilson (Lambertville, NJ., 1988), 356. The estate was purchased by Robert Morris for his daughter and son-in-law. Elisabeth M. Nuxoll, "Illegitimacy, Family Status and Property in the Early Republic: The Morris-Croxall Family of New Jersey," *New Jersey History*, 113 (fall/winter 1995, nos. 3-4), 6, 17 n11.

Robert Hoops was elected a delegate in 1787 from Sussex County to the New Jersey State Convention called to ratify the Federal Constitution and was a candidate for Congress from New Jersey in 1789. *Pennsylvania Packet and Daily Advertiser*, December 29, 1787; "Notes and Queries," PMHB, 11 (1887): 501-02.

[61] Deed dated March 26, 1770 for 320 acres purchased from the Hezekiah Anderson estate by Adam Hoops, Bucks County Deed Book 13, p. 239; Terry A. McNealy,

(continued...)

Martic Foundry and Forge in Lancaster.[62]   He bought farmland in Bedford County and continued to add to his already considerable property in Cumberland County.[63]   He built grist mills, bolting mills, and saw mills, and developed fishing both at Summerseat and at the estate Belvidere in New Jersey.

His largest land venture was in Nova Scotia. In 1765 he was one of five grantees awarded 100,000 acres along the Petitcodiac River in Hopewell Township on the Bay of Fundy. His fellow proprietors were the Swiss officers, Colonel Frederick Haldimand and newly-promoted Brigadier General Henry Bouquet, German-born Peter Hasenclever, and New York merchant Hugh Wallace.[64]   Adam

---

[61](...continued)
comp., *Bucks County Sheriffs' Deeds, 1749-1776* (Doylestown, 1989), #138.

[62] Franklin Ellis, *History of Lancaster County, Pennsylvania,* 2 vols. (1883; Lancaster, 1986), 2:976; National Society of the Colonial Dames of America, Pennsylvania, *Forges and Furnaces in the Province of Pennsylvania* (Philadelphia, 1914), 139.

[63] Land warrants in Adam Hoops's name date from 1749. They are: #479, August 7, 1749 for 100 acres in Lancaster County (this part of Lancaster became Cumberland County in 1750); #5, April 13, 1751 for 200 acres in Antrim Township, Cumberland County; #7, September 30, 1751 for 50 acres in Antrim Township, Cumberland County; #20, August 25, 1753 for 100 acres in Hopewell Township, Cumberland County; #21, September 7, 1753 for 50 acres in Hopewell Township, Cumberland County; #23, April 12, 1754 for 50 acres in Guilford Township, Cumberland County; #24, April 13, 1754 for 20 acres in Guilford Township, Cumberland County; #47, July 2, 1756 for lot #173 in Carlisle, Cumberland County; #82, June 9, 1762 for 300 acres "on both sides of the Shawanese Cabbin Creek," Cumberland County; #136, May 30, 1763 for 304 acres in Hopewell Township, Cumberland County; #142, October 5, 1764 for 210 acres "near" the town of Carlisle on both sides of LeTort's Spring, Cumberland County; #143, March 14, 1765 for 479 1/8 acres in Hopewell Township, Cumberland County; #169, December 23, 1766 for 50 acres in Guilford Township, Cumberland County; #170, January 7, 1767 for 250 acres in Peters Township, Cumberland County; and #176, February 18, 1767 for 200 acres in Letterkenny Township, Cumberland County. All of these warrants were copied from microfilm entitled *Pennsylvania-Land and Property. Original Warrants, Lancaster County, H-286,* reel #1028747, and *Original Warrants, Cumberland County, F-121 to H-415,* reel #1028719, available through the Church of Jesus Christ of Latter Day Saints' Family History Centers. See also PA, 3rd ser., 24:434, 684-88; Merri Lou Scribner Schaumann, *Tax Lists - Cumberland County, Pennsylvania, 1750, 1751, 1752, 1753, 1762, 1763, 1764* (Wellsville, Pa., 1974), 3, 14, 16, 18, 23, 40, 45, 62, 66, and *Tax Lists - Cumberland County, Pennsylvania, 1768, 1769, 1770* (Carlisle, 1972), 35, 42, 84, 113, 117, 120, 151. For Hoops's property in Bedford County, see PA, 3rd ser., 22:62, 94, 211.

[64] Crown Land Grants, Old Book 5, pp.400-02 (call number 13036) and Old Book
(continued...)

Hoops sailed to Nova Scotia in September 1765 to inspect the lands, to check on the fertility of the soil and to sign the grant on behalf of his fellow proprietors. Advice from Peter Hasenclever and Hugh Wallace to him included the instructions "to proceed to have it surveyed, & care taken to take up none but good Lands, as bad Lands wont pay the Quit Rent...."[65] Evidently, the lands passed his inspection, as upon his return to Philadelphia Hoops began immediately taking an active interest in the settlement, finding farmers, moving their families there, hiring the manager, shipping them cattle, tools, and supplies. Two years later he was receiving fruits of their labor, potatoes, cheeses and plaster of Paris from a local quarry.[66]

---

[64](...continued)
6, pp. 377-79 (call number 13035), Public Archives of Nova Scotia. On microfilm. A manuscript copy of this grant is also in the Bank of New York Archives, One Wall Street, New York 10286.

[65] Peter Hasenclever and Hugh Wallace to Adam Hoops, New York 25th July 1765, File Folder 4, Bank of New York Archives, 10th floor, One Wall Street, New York 10286.

[66] Considerable documentation exists on this Nova Scotia land grant, due primarily to a lawsuit filed by the planters against the proprietors in October 1771 (after Adam Hoops's death). Canadian scholar Esther Clark Wright researched pre-Loyalist Nova Scotia land grants and published the results in *The Petitcodiac: a Study of the New Brunswick River and of the people who settled along it* (Sackville, N. B., [1945] and *Planters and Pioneers* (Hantsport, N.S., 1978). There is much on Hopewell Township and Adam Hoops. Since Dr. Wright's studies appeared, there was discovered in 1981 at the Bank of New York on Wall Street a cache of old documents relating to this Nova Scotia land grant. Although information on this collection is available through the RLIN database, none of the documents have been catalogued, indexed, or microfilmed.   The cache consists of twelve folders of miscellaneous papers ranging in date from 1764 to 1830, two sketch maps, account books, and a ledger. Thanks to the kindness and generosity of Consulting Archivist Christine McKay, we list a sample from this rich trove of unconsulted documents:
   Folder 2 - Article of Agreement between Joseph Richards and the Proprietors Colonel Frederick Haldimand, Peter Hasenclever, Hugh Wallace and Adam Hoops, dated 5 February 1766 at Philadelphia for 200 acres of land "at or near Germantown" in Hopewell Township, Nova Scotia.
   Folder 3 - Copy of the grant by Montagu Wilmot, Governor of Province of Nova Scotia, awarding 100,000 acres to the five proprietors in Hopewell Township, dated Halifax September 24, 1765, and countersigned for the proprietors by Hugh Wallace; Copy of the Terms of settling the land, i.e. "Ye Number of Settlers be in Proportion of one family for every four Hundred Acres," unsigned and undated (c. April 1765).
   Folder 4 - Article of Agreement between Caspar Seizlar and the Proprietors, dated 5 February 1766 at Philadelphia, for two hundred acres in Hopewell Township;
                                                                                (continued...)

66(...continued)
Article of Agreement between Adam Ling and the Proprietors, dated 15 February 1766 at Philadelphia for two hundred acres in Hopewell Township; Article of Agreement between George Lee and the Proprietors, dated 22 February 1766 at Philadelphia for two hundred acres in Hopewell Township; Letter to Adam Hoops from Charles Baker, Germantown, Nova Scotia, 21 October 1766 re surveying the township at Hoops's request; Letter to Adam Hoops from Moses Delesderniers, Hillsborough in Nova Scotia, 15th Feby 1769; Letter to Adam Hoops from Robert Cummins, his nephew, Nova Scotia, 21 October 1766; Statement of Accounts, "Nova Scotia Estate Hopewell Township To Brigadier General Haldimand or Hugh Wallace Attorney for Brigadier General Haldimand" concerning a debt of Peter Hasenclever paid by General Haldimand, 29 January 1766; Copy of the "Minute of a Council holden at Halifax on the 8th of August 1764" regarding application for 1000 acres each from Lieut. Desbarres "in behalf of Colonel Bouquet, Colonel Fredk Haldimand, Mr Shillwell & Mr Peter deVisme & others." (On the outside of this document is the notation, "We are threatned with the Paper Stamp Duty, therefore you had better contrive to send some families immediately and I shall contrive to get out the Patent as soon as I can prove to the Council that you are actually serious in improving the Lands..."); Judgement by a Boston Court in favor of four sailors of the schooner *Rose* out of Philadelphia and shipwrecked off the coast of Cape Cod, who sued Captain Samuel Snell, master, for their wages, December 10 & 11, 1766; Copy of a letter to Colonel Bouquet from Lieut. Desbarres, Halifax 28 April 1765; Letter to Adam Hoops from Charles Baker, Germantown, Nova Scotia, 27 September 1766, surveying the township lands; and a Letter to Adam Hoops from Hugh Wallace, New York, 10 August 1765, saying he is sending a large map of Nova Scotia, with the advice to "get it carefully pasted on Linnen, to prevent its being damaged, any of your Picture Frame-makers know how to do it." Interested persons may contact the Bank of New York Archives, 10th floor, One Wall Street, New York 10286 for further details.

There are also important letters pertaining to this land grant in The Haldimand Papers, British Museum, Additional Manuscripts 21,728, Letters of 1757-1768, photostat copies in LC. Letters from Adam Hoops to General Haldimand are calendared in the *Catalogue of Additions to the Manuscripts in the British Museum, in the Years MDCCCLIV-MDCCCLX* (London, 1875), Additional MSS, 21,728, p. 505. See also the entry for Sir Frederick Haldimand in the *Dictionary of Canadian Biography*, 5: 887-904.

In the National Archives of Canada Finding Aid 92 lists references to Adam Hoops and the Hopewell Township: MG 23, D 1, Series I: Lawrence Collection, General Correspondence, Letters received, Ward Chipman Senior, Vol. 1, Freeman, Edwd. (1769), on microfilm reel C-1179; and "Hopewell - Grant to Henry Bouquet, Frederick Haldimand, Hugh Wallis, Peter Hassenclever, Adam Hoops, & associates, 1765, as well as other papers such as supporting papers, list of bonds, etc. on pp. 86-145," on microfilm reel C-13151. See also the Ward Chipman Papers, MG 23, D 1, Series I :Lawrence Collection: Papers Relative to Townships and Settlements, Records Relating to Saint John City, and County and to various settlements in New Brunswick, 1765-1842 (volumes 10-11), on microfilm reel C-13151.

The extent of Adam Hoops's investment in Hopewell Township at the time of his death is unclear. There is no mention of these lands in his will. Yet, the

(continued...)

Adam Hoops had risen far from his whiskey keg-making days on the Pennsylvania frontier. When he had returned from a year in Europe in 1764 the *Pennsylvania Journal* noted the arrival of the ship *Catherine* from Liverpool "in whom came Passenger Mr. Adam Hoops and his Family."[67] Like other wealthy merchants of the time, Adam Hoops contributed to charitable institutions, supported his church, and signed the Non-Importation Agreement in 1765.[68] His contributions to the Pennsylvania Hospital, and to the Academy at Philadelphia were noted in the Pennsylvania newspapers.[69] He was active in Presbyterian Church affairs in Carlisle, Lancaster, and

[66](...continued)
correspondence cited above leads us to believe he was still a shareholder at his death. Further study of all documents in the above-cited repositories may provide clarification.

As to the industry of the Hopewell Township settlers, the record of their exports speaks for itself. Samples of potatoes, cheese, and plaster of Paris were sent to Adam Hoops in 1767 (two years after the first settlers arrived). He thought the plaster "very good and shall send a sample of it to England to see if a Market can be found there." (Hoops to Haldimand, Summersett 23d Augst 1767, The Haldimand Papers, British Museum Additional MSS 21,728. Pt. IV, photostats in LC). It indeed was good, and the export continued and expanded. In 1799 in the *New Jersey Gazette* a merchant was advertising the arrival "Fresh from the Quarry and warranted of the first quality, 40 tons Nova-Scotia PLASTER..." (*New Jersey Gazette*, June 18, 1799). In 1945 Dr. Wright noted in her book that "gypsum, from which various grades of plaster are manufactured," was still being quarried and exported. She further noted, "To Hopewell must go the honour of the first recorded export of New Brunswick potatoes, the principal agricultural export of the province at the present." (Wright, *The Petitcodiac*, 31-32).

[67] *Pennsylvania Journal*, June 14, 1764.

[68] "Facsimile of the Autographs of the Merchants and other Citizens of Philadelphia as subscribed to the Non-Importation Resolutions, October 25th, 1765," Frank M. Etting, *An Historical Account of the Old State House of Pennsylvania now known as the Hall of Independence*, 2nd ed. (Philadelphia, 1891),between pages 51 & 52, also Appendix A, where Adam Hoops's name is mistakenly given as Andrew, 208. Printed also in Thomas Willing Balch, *Willing Letters and Papers Edited With a Biographical Essay of Thomas Willing of Philadelphia (1731-1821)* (Philadelphia, 1922), 37.

[69] The *Pennsylvania Gazette* of July 15, 1762 lists a contribution to the Pennsylvania Hospital of £30 from Adam Hoops and in the April 23, 1761 issue of the *Pennsylvania Journal* Hoops is listed as the manager in Carlisle for lottery tickets for the "Benefit of the College, Academy and Charitable Schools of Philadelphia."

Philadelphia[70] and was an early donor to the Juliana Library in Lancaster.[71] His name was on the *Pennsylvania Journal* customer list in 1764 for two subscriptions.[72] For the two years before his death he also served as justice of the peace in Bucks County.[73] He may also have been a benefactor to Benjamin West, the artist (see Appendix A).

Unlike other wealthy merchants, Hoops did not change his religion to the socially acceptable Anglican faith. His name does not appear in the dancing assembly lists or in the Mt. Regale Fishing Club and Gloucester Hunting Club rosters.[74] There are no ball and claw furniture or gilded-framed portraits in Summerseat's extensive inventory (reproduced in Appendix B). There are, though, 78 Windsor chairs, four old Indian blankets, "6 Roman Antiquities, General

[70] *Pennsylvania Gazette*, July 2, 1761, and June 24, 1762; Allan D. Thompson, *The Meeting House on the Square: an Historical Sketch of the First Presbyterian Church of Carlisle, Pennsylvania*, 30-31; Thomas Clinton Pears, Jr., Notes on pew rolls of First Presbyterian and Old Pine Street Presbyterian Churches, Philadelphia, 1747-1791, n.d., MS P316nf; and Records [of the] First Presbyterian Church, Philadelphia, 1747-1772, typewritten pages in file folder, 114, 140-142, both in Presbyterian Historical Society library, Philadelphia. Hoops was one of six chosen by the Corporation for the Relief of Poor and Distressed Presbyterian Ministers and for the Frontier Inhabitants to attend Indian treaty negotiations at Lancaster in August 1762. Photostatic copy of Ms. Minutes of the Corporation for the Relief of Poor and Distressed Presbyterian Ministers...pp. 37-41, quoted by Guy Soulliard Klett, ed., *Journals of Charles Beatty, 1762-1769* (University Park, 1962), 33 n.28.

[71] Charles I. Landis, "The Juliana Library Company in Lancaster," *Historical Papers and Addresses of the Lancaster County Historical Society* (Lancaster, Pa., 1929), 33:213.

[72] "A List of the Customers Town & Country A.D. 1764 of The Pennsylvania Journal Published in Philadelphia by Col. William Bradford," MS in William Bradford Papers, HSP.

[73] PA, 2nd ser., 9:768.

[74] Thomas Willing Balch, *The Philadelphia Assemblies* (Philadelphia, 1916); "The Mount Regale Fishing Company of Philadelphia," *PMHB*, 27 (1903):88-90, lists members for the years 1762 and 1763 only; [William Milner], *Memoirs of the Gloucester Fox Hunting Club near Philadelphia* (Philadelphia, 1830), 7, where members for the organizational year of 1766 are given. Although one cannot picture former frontiersman Adam Hoops at a dancing assembly, his daughters and daughter-in-law attended one, if the list of names Thomas Balch published on pp. 69-75 is in fact one such assembly. The Mrs. Hoops is surely son Robert's wife, née Martha Cottnam, married in March 1771, Mrs. Mease is James's wife, née Isabel Hoops and Miss P. Hoops is Margaret ("Peggy") Hoops (all on p.75). Margaret Hoops married in September 1772, so this list can be dated between March 1771 and September 1772. The Mrs. Barclay listed on p. 70 may be Thomas's wife, Mary; if so, another Hoops daughter attended.

Monctons Picture & Cleopatra."[75] As a poorly educated self-made man, Hoops was, we suspect, not that socially acceptable to the elite of Philadelphia, although his money was. His children married well, but they did not marry sons and daughters of prominent Philadelphia families.[76] It is rare to find him mentioned in personal letters or social commentary of the period, although we hope this study will bring to light such correspondence.[77]   It is in death only that he made Elizabeth Drinker's well-known diary.[78]

When he died in June 1771 Adam Hoops owned over 3000 acres of land in Pennsylvania, New Jersey, and Maryland, as well as a one-fifth share in a Nova Scotia township.[79]   At a time when a man was considered wealthy if he had between £20,000-£35,000, Hoops's estate was valued at £42,079.[80]   Adam Hoops's wealth has escaped the study of business historians perhaps because no account books or letterbooks have been found, although judging from a direct reference to them in one Hoops letter, they obviously existed at one time.[81]

[75] Will no.79, 1771, Office of the Recorder of Wills, Philadelphia City Hall. Listed also in Richard T. & Mildred C. Williams, comps., *Index of Wills & Administration Records, Philadelphia, Pennsylvania, 1682-1782* (Danboro, PA, 1971-72), 87.

[76] Jane, Isabel and Mary married Irish-born immigrants, while Sarah, Margaret and David married into Virginia families. Robert married a daughter of a New Jersey lawyer and Adam Jr., as far as we know, remained unmarried.

[77] The one letter we located shows he was known and consulted in the community. Daniel Clark is writing on behalf of his father-in-law to Dr. Jonathan Potts, "Mr Hoops being just now bled is unable himself to write but desires I will acquaint you that since you left him this Evening he talked to Doctor Harris on the Subject of your Differences, and that he is in hopes to Succeed in accommodating maters between you to morrow, and he requests you will be pleased to call upon him at his House at 9 o clock tomorrow morning." This undated letter is addressed "To Doctor Jonathan Potts at Mr Clement Biddles." The probable date is between late 1768, when Daniel Clark returned to Philadelphia from west Florida, and June, 1771, the month Hoops died. The Papers of Dr. Jonathan Potts, vol. 1, 1766-1776, HSP.

[78] "Genealogical Gleanings from the Journal of Elizabeth Drinker, 1759-1807," *Pennsylvania Vital Records From the Pennsylvania Genealogical Magazine and the Pennsylvania Magazine of History and Biography*, (Baltimore, 1966), 1:592.

[79] Will no.79, 1771. Office of the Recorder of Wills, Philadelphia City Hall. *Pennsylvania Gazette*, April 30, 1772.

[80] Thomas M. Doerflinger, *A Vigorous Spirit of Enterprise*, 25-26. 128-29. Compare Hoops's net worth with two of his contemporaries in ibid., Table 10 on p. 130.

[81] "My Letter Books and my memorandoms are all at Somerseat...," Adam Hoops to General Haldimand, Philadelphia, June 10, 1768, The Haldimand Papers, British

(continued...)

Adam Hoops was a resident of Philadelphia only a few years, from 1761 to 1771, and part of that time he was at Summerseat. He owned a chariot, but this ownership fell between the dates of the two lists of carriage owners usually cited by scholars on wealthy Philadelphia merchants.[82] He is on the Philadelphia tax lists of 1767 and 1769, but this does not show his real wealth, because most of his property holdings were outside the city of Philadelphia.[83] A more meaningful indication of his net worth is found in his will and associated account of his estate, the extensive inventory of Summerseat, and the lengthy list of his properties advertised for sale in the *Pennsylvania Gazette* of April 30, 1772.[84] (reproduced in Appendix C).

After Hoops's death, his family continued living at Summerseat until the estate was cleared up and the will probated. Then the estate was put up for sale.

To Be Sold - A plantation and tract of land, called

---

[81](...continued)
Museum Additional MSS 21728, Pt. 7, photostats at LC.

[82] "An Account of Coaches, Landaus, Chariots, and Four-Wheel Chaises in Philadelphia, 1761," PMHB, 27:375; Robert F. Oaks, "Big Wheels in Philadelphia: Du Simitière's List of Carriage Owners," PMHB, 95 (July, 1971): 351-62. Hoops may not have owned a chariot when the first list was compiled, as he did not move to Philadelphia until May of 1761. Du Simitière's list was compiled in 1772, by which time Adam Hoops had died. In his will dated June 7, 1771, Hoops bequeathed to "my said beloved wife my chariot, furniture and two horses belonging thereto." Will no.79, 1771, Office of the Recorder of Wills, Philadelphia City Hall.

[83] Transcript of the Assessment for the 1767 Provincial Tax for the City and County of Philadelphia, Mulberry Ward, p. 200, Rare Book Room, Van Pelt Library, University of Pennsylvania, microfilm copy; PA, 3rd ser., 14: 207. Hoops was a resident of Mulberry Ward, where he is listed as "Adam Hope, merch't." His name has been variously transcribed as Hope, Hoope, Hoopes, and even Hoak. Although one must be cautious about assuming that "Adam Hope" is indeed this Adam Hoops, in this case we can be certain. The two Adam Hopes listed in the PA index did not live in Philadelphia. One was a weaver in Chester County in 1766, the other—the same person?—a farmer in York County in 1779.

[84]Copies of Adam Hoops's will are in the Historical Society of Pennsylvania (Bucks County Box) and in the National Archives of Canada (Ward Chipman Papers: Records of Various Townships and Settlements in New Brunswick, 1765-1829, MG 23, D 1, Series 1, volume 10, pp. 101-107, microfilm reel C-13 151). It is also printed in Eugenia G. Glazebrook and Preston G. Glazebrook, comps., *Virginia Migrations Hanover County*, (Richmond, 1949), 2 (1743-1871):64-66. The original will, Summerseat inventory, and estate accounts are in the Office of the Recorder of Wills, Philadelphia City Hall, Will no.79, 1771.

Summerseat, pleasantly situated on the river Delaware, near the falls of Trenton, in the county of Bucks, containing 220 acres, or thereabouts, of which 125 acres are clear, including 40 acres of good meadow, the rest woodland; there is a large new and well finished brick house, kitchen, stone barn, stables, and other offices erected on the premises—also two young orchards, and two dwelling houses, at one of which is kept a store, the whole in good repair. At this place is caught, in the season, great quantities of shad, herring, sturgeon, rock, and perch; its situation renders it one of the most agreeable seats on Delaware, being at the head of the tide-water, only 29 miles from Philadelphia, and not 100 yards from the post road between the latter and New-York....[85]

Interested buyers were requested to make enquiries to "Mrs. Elizabeth Hoops, Robert or David Hoops at Summerseat, near Trenton Ferry, to Daniel Clarke at Clover Hill, or to Thomas Barclay in Philadelphia."[86]

---

[85] The advertisement continues: "A town at this place is much wished for, and the purchaser may lay out a few acres in lots, to the greatest advantage in that part which lies most contiguous to the ferry. An island, containing 40 acres of excellent land; and 20 acres opposite thereto, and adjoining the above described plantation, whereon is erected a compleat merchant mill, 60 x 54 feet, accommodated with one pair of burr, one pair of Cologne, and one pair of country stones, with scales and weights, a rolling screen, boulting works and hoisting geers, all going by water. A handsome two story frame dwelling house, a kitchen, stone stable, and barn;—two stone tenements, which may lett for Fifteen Pounds per annum;—a smith's shop, with bellows, anvil, and other necessary tools. A sloop, that carries 320 barrels of flour, may load within 200 yards of the mill tail. This mill has the advantage of being almost fully supplied with wheat from Durham and the Minisinks, as the boats may, without passing through the falls, come into the dam, and deliver their grain almost at the mill door." *Pennsylvania Gazette*, April 30, 1772. The same ad with slightly different wording appeared in the *Pennsylvania Journal, and the Weekly Advertiser* of October 14, 1772 with the additional information that Summerseat "will be sold peremptorily at PUBLIC VENDUE, on the premises, the 10th day of November next."

[86] Elizabeth Finney Hoops, born 1720, died July 19, 1782 in Philadelphia had five daughters and three sons by Adam Hoops. Buried in Bank Street Presbyterian Churchyard, her remains were removed to Laurel Hill Cemetery in 1846. Her will, dated July 18, 1782, is in the Office of the Recorder of Wills, Philadelphia City Hall, Will no.143, 1782. The one letter written by her reveals her to be a fond grand-mother. Elizabeth Hoops to Thomas Walker, Jr., November 21, 1780, Thomas Walker Papers in the William Cabell Rives Papers, Microfilm Reel 2, container 162, LC.

(continued...)

86(...continued)

Robert Hoops, 1745-1818, oldest son of Adam and Elizabeth Hoops, attended the University of Pennsylvania in 1758, married Martha Cottnam of Trenton, 1771, was elected deputy commissary-general of issues in 1777 during the Revolution, served as brigade major to General Philemon Dickinson and died without issue in Hamilton, New York in his 73rd year. Thomas H. Montgomery, *A History of the University of Pennsylvania from its Foundation to A.D. 1770* (Philadelphia, 1900), 540; Hamilton Schuyler, *A History of St. Michael's Church Trenton* (Princeton, 1926), 393-94; *Journals of the Continental Congress* (hereafter JCC), 8:517; Edmund C. Burnett, ed., *Letters of Members of the Continental Congress* (Washington, 1923), 2:408; 412; Letter from Robert Hoops to General Horatio Gates, January 26, 1783, Gates Papers, Box 16, #155, New York Historical Society Manuscript Dept.; Charles E. Claghorn, *Women Patriots of the American Revolution: a biographical dictionary* (Metuchen, N.J., 1991), 105; George Wyckoff Cummins, *History of Warren County New Jersey* (New York, 1911), 44, 112-14, 117, 214; Frank Dale, *Delaware Diary: Episodes in the Life of a River* (New Brunswick, NJ, 1996), 21, 35; Jay C. Richards, *Penn, Patriots and The Pequest: The History of Pre-Victorian Belvidere: 1716 to 1845* (Belvidere,, NJ, 1995), 19-28, 40-42, 44-45; *History of Cattaraugus County, New York* (Philadelphia, 1879), 30, 153-54, 169, 170-71; *Times, and New-Brunswick General Advertiser* (New Jersey), October 1, 1818.

David Hoops, 1748/49-18--?, second son of Adam and Elizabeth Hoops, also attended the University of Pennsylvania, married Mildred Syme in Virginia in c1775, had two sons, and became a widower in 1779. Both sons, one of whom was named John Syme Hoops, had died by 1804. Efforts to trace David Hoops after 1812, when he was left some money in his sister Jane Clark's will, have proved futile. Thomas H. Montgomery, *A History of the University of Pennsylvania from its Foundation to A.D. 1770*, 540; Donald Jackson, ed., *The Diaries of George Washington*, 6 vols. (Charlottesville, 1978), 3:106; Eugenia G. Glazebrook and Preston G. Glazebrook, comps., *Virginia Migrations Hanover County, 1743-1871*, 2:xiii, xv, 71-76; *The Papers of James Madison* , various editors, 17 vols. (Chicago & Charlottesville, 1962-1991), 1:141-45; "Record of Servants and Apprentices Bound and Assigned before Hon. John Gibson, Mayor of Philadelphia, December 5th, 1772-May 21, 1773," PMHB, 34 (1910):220; Malcolm Harris, *History of Louisa County, Virginia* (Richmond, 1936), 162; Will and Inventory of Jane Clark, deceased, Will no. 111, 1812, Office of the Recorder of Wills, Philadelphia City Hall.

Daniel Clark, 1732-1800, Irish born, fought in the French-Indian War, where he was a lieutenant in Major James Burd's company of the Third Battalion at Fort Augusta in 1756-57. He married Jane Hoops in 1758, was associated with his father-in-law in Carlisle in the provisioning business until he moved to Philadelphia in 1761. He tried the merchant life for a few years, went to west Florida in 1765 to look into the land grant awarded veterans of the French-Indian Wars, served as assistant to the governor in Mobile for a while, returned to Philadelphia in late 1768 or early 1769. He and Jane lived in Bucks County until he sold that estate in 1773 to move to Natchez territory. Back in Philadelphia in the early 1780s, Clark was agent for Robert Morris's tobacco contract, working in Virginia in 1783 and 1784. Shortly thereafter, he moved to Mississippi territory to manage his 5,000 acre land grant, where his many letters and relations with his nephew of the same name can be found in the Winthrop Sargent Papers in the Massachusetts Historical Society. Contrary to

(continued...)

In 1773, Thomas Barclay purchased 221 acres "and 83 perches," the bulk of the Summerseat property, from the estate of his father-in-law.[87] It seems reasonable to assume that Barclay had in mind the increase of his family when he decided to purchase Summerseat. It was in October 1773 that his first child and daughter was born.[88]

---

[86](...continued)
written accounts, Daniel Clark did not die a wealthy man. He was deeply in debt the last years of his life, living on an annuity arranged by his nephew. After Clark died on July 16, 1800 (not 1799 as some writers have it), his widow returned to Philadelphia, where she lived until her death in 1812. PA, 5th ser., 1:46-47, 62-63, 70-71, 92; "Military Letters of Captain Joseph Shippen of the Provincial Service, 1756-1758," PMHB, 36 (1912): 408,417-18, 424-25, 434, 436-41; Thomas Balch, ed., *Letters and Papers Relating Chiefly to the Provincial History of Pennsylvania with some Notices of the Writers* (Philadelphia, 1855), 69-70, 98, 100-101, 102; Nicholas B. Wainwright, *George Croghan: Wilderness Diplomat* (Chapel Hill, 1959), 196-99; Burd-Shippen Papers, APS; Provincial Council Records, 1760-1768, Exhibits 2 & 4, June 2, 1763, HSP; Indenture between George Croghan and William Peters & Daniel Clark, June 2, 1763, Society Collections, HSP; A. T. Volwiler, "George Croghan and the Westward Movement, 1741-1782," PMHB, 46 (1922):280; Daniel Clark Letterbook, 1759-1761, HSP; Winston De Ville, *English Land Grants in West Florida: A Register for the States of Alabama, Mississippi, and Parts of Florida and Louisiana, 1766-1776*, (Ville Platte, La., 1986), 8-9, 10,11,14; Daniel Clark letter to Baynton, Wharton & Morgan, Philadelphia, April 28, 1764, Baynton Wharton & Morgan Papers, microfilm roll 3, frame 959, Pennsylvania State Archives; Billie Ford Snider and Janice B. Palmer, comps., *Spanish Plat Book of Land Records of the District of Pensacola, Province of West Florida: British and Spanish Land Grants, 1763-1821* (Pensacola, 1994), 226,228, 230,510, 511, 517; E. James Ferguson, ed., *The Papers of Robert Morris*, many letters and references in vols. 2, 4,5,6,7, 8 (see "Daniel Clark" in index); William Nelson, ed., *Documents Relating to the Colonial History of the State of New Jersey*, Tenth Volume of Extracts from American Newspapers Relating to New Jersey, 1773-1774, (Paterson, N.J., 1917), 1st ser., 29:5; Norman E. Gillis, *Early Inhabitants of the Natchez District* ([Baton Rouge? La.], 1963), 7, 15; Dunbar Rowland, ed., *Mississippi Comprising Sketches of Counties, Towns, Events, Institutions, and Persons Arranged in Cyclopedic Form*, 3 vols (Atlanta, 1907), 1: 304, 445-46; 2: 36, 38, 240, 304, 395-96; William S. Coker and Jack D. L. Holmes, eds., "Daniel Clark's Letter on the Mississippi Territory," *Journal of Mississippi History*, 32 (1970): 153-69; Jack D. L. Holmes, "Cotton Gins in the Spanish Natchez District, 1795-1800," *Journal of Mississippi History*, 31.162-63, 168-70; Lawrence Kinnaird, ed., *Annual Report of the American Historical Association for the Year 1945*, Volume 3 (Pt. 2): Spain in the Mississippi Valley, 1765-1794, Part 2: Post War Decade, 1782-1791 (Washington, 1946), 263-64, 305-07; Frederick S. Allis, Jr., ed., *Guide to the Microfilm Edition of the Winthrop Sargent Papers* (Boston, 1965), 41 (where many letters of Daniel Clark are listed).

[87] Bucks County Deed book 16, pp. 226-228, dated April 30, 1773, recorded June 8, 1774. He paid £2010.

[88] Elizabeth Mease Barclay, 1773-1832, went to France with her parents in 1781, returned to Philadelphia in 1788, moved to Virginia with her mother in 1791, when

(continued...)

SUMMERSEAT IN HISTORY

Summerseat's week of fame came in December 1776. George Washington really did sleep there. Historians think he slept there for six nights, possibly seven. No Barclay family correspondence has been found to corroborate Washington's imprecise letter headings. None of the published diaries and journals kept by Washington, his aides or his generals include entries for this week.[89] Only two personal letters have been located that may have been written at Summerseat between December 8 and 14.[90] However, from a careful reading of the letters of General Washington, his military aides, his secretaries, and those from Congress, we can reconstruct the week George Washington lived at "Mr. Berkleys Summer Seat."

The disastrous defeat of the American troops by the British and Hessians in three New York campaigns in 1776—Long Island in August, White Plains in October, and Fort Washington in November—and the retreat of this "apology of an army" across New Jersey

---

[88](...continued)
her father went abroad on another diplomatic mission, married Peyton Randolph Harrison of the James River Harrisons in 1795, moved to Kentucky in 1809, suffered 17 pregnancies and bore nine children, of whom two survived her. She died in Russellville, Logan County, Kentucky in 1832. Sixty of her letters written between the years 1800 and 1831 are in the Virginia Historical Society in the Papers of the Harrison Family (Mss1/H248/c) and four letters written between the years 1808-1829 are in the Bethany College Archives (Dr. James Barclay Donaldson bequest), Bethany, West Virginia. R. Burnham Moffatt, *The Barclays of New York: Who They Are and Who They Are Not, - and Some Other Barclays* (New York, 1904), 234; Anna Mary Moon, comp., *Sketches of the Moon and Barclay Families Including the Harris, Moorman, Johnson, Appling Families* (Chattanooga, 1939),70-71; *Virginia Magazine of History and Biography*, 35(January 1927):209.

[89] The following were checked: Donald Jackson, ed., *Diaries of George Washington,* (Charlottesville, 1976-1979), 6 vols.; Worthington C. Ford, ed., *Correspondence and Journals of Samuel Blachley Webb*, 3 vols. (1893; New York, 1969), vol. 1, 1772-1777; Samuel A. Harrison, ed., *Memoir of Lieut. Col. Tench Tilghman*, (1876, New York, 1971); Richard K. Showman, ed., *The Papers of General Nathanael Greene*, 6 vols. (Chapel Hill, 1976), 1: December 1766-December 1776; The Papers of Adam Stephen, 1749-1849, MS 17, 126, LC. Microfilm.

[90] George Washington to Lund Washington, Falls of Delaware, South Side, December 10, 1776, *The Writings of George Washington from the Original Manuscript Sources, 1745-1799*, John C. Fitzpatrick, ed., 39 vols. (Washington, 1931-44), 6:345-46; Colonel Henry Knox to Mrs. Lucy Knox, "Trenton Ferry abt 30 miles from Philadelphia Dec 8, 1776," Henry Knox Papers on microfilm, Massachusetts Historical Society. The original Henry Knox Papers are now on deposit at the Pierpont Morgan Library, New York, as part of the Gilder Lehrman Collection.

have been vividly told and heroically retold in numerous books.[91]
We all know the story of the Battle of Trenton, how General
Washington and his ragged troops crossed the ice-clogged Delaware
on a cold Christmas Day of 1776, and snatched a victory from the
unsuspecting Hessians. "Those final hours of 1776 and the opening
days of 1777 were, in many respects, the finest of George
Washington's military career," wrote one historian.[92] This fine old
mansion, Summerseat, "one of the most agreeable seats on [the]
Delaware," shared in the honor and glory of those final hours.

The exertions of getting his troops safely across New Jersey and
into Pennsylvania out of the clutches of the British and Hessians, the
continuing attrition of his army through enlistment terminations and
desertions, and the constant second-guessing of General Howe's
movements left no time for personal letters or idle jottings in a diary.
"I am in Haste...," wrote Washington from Trenton on December 7.[93]
And in haste he was. After initial dallying, General Howe was
pursuing the Americans with a vigor that he had not previously
shown. On November 20 Washington was at Hackensack, New
Jersey, his army of about 2000 divided into four fragments. Howe
was marching rapidly with his army of 6000 on their way to cross the
Hudson. On November 21 Washington was in Passaic. On November
23 he was in Newark. Although bad weather slowed the British,
they began to move on November 27. The next day General
Washington marched out of Newark, as General Howe marched in.
The British and Hessians were by this time 12,000 strong.[94]

The Continental Army, on the other hand, was 2,000 weak, and
getting weaker. Douglas S. Freeman, the biographer of George
Washington, said it eloquently when he wrote,

---

[91] William S. Stryker, *The Battles of Trenton and Princeton*, (Boston, 1898); Douglas
S. Freeman, *George Washington, A Biography*, 7 vols. (New York, 1948-1957), vol.
4; Samuel Stelle Smith, *The Battle of Trenton* (Monmouth Beach, N.J.,1965); William
M. Dwyer, *The Day is Ours! November 1776-January 1777: An Inside View of the
Battles of Trenton and Princeton* (New York, 1983); Thomas Fleming, *1776: Year of
Illusions* (New York, 1975), 457-69; Richard M. Ketchum, *The Winter Soldiers*,
(Garden City, NY, 1973); and Robert K. Wright, Jr., *The Continental Army*
(Washington, 1989), 94-98.

[92] Richard M. Ketchum, *The World of George Washington*, (New York, 1973), 111.

[93] George Washington to Major General William Heath, Trenton, December 7, 1776,
John C. Fitzpatrick, ed., *The Writings of George Washington*, 6:335.

[94] William S. Stryker, *The Battles of Trenton and Princeton*, 8-9.

> The poor American army kept dwindling in a manner to
> make a stout heart stop beating...exhortation, oratory and
> the tender of the bounty had weighed not at all against fear
> and cold, homesickness and the professed belief that the
> other man ought now to do his part.[95]

General Washington marched on. On November 29 the
Americans reached Brunswick. Confidently, the commander in chief
awaited the coming of General Charles Lee's 3000 troops.[96] With or
without Lee, the British had to be stopped. In Trenton on December
3rd General Washington turned his attention to the Delaware River.[97]
The river was to be scoured the length of its navigable stretch above
Philadelphia—seventy miles north—collecting every boat in the water
and even those rotting under the water. Not one was to be left for the
British to find and resurrect.[98]

General Howe, hoping to overtake what one American Loyalist
described as "half starved, half clothed, half armed, discontented,
ungovernable, undisciplined wretches,"[99]pressed on with the intention
of cutting them down before they crossed the Delaware, but between
December 3 and 6, the British troops under Major General Corn-
wallis halted. General Howe, evidently more intent on finding a comfortable place for winter quarters than on pursuing the enemy,
ordered them "not to advance beyond Brunswick."[100]

This respite gave Washington time to get his sick and injured
troops, stores and baggage wagons across the Delaware on December
5. The sick and injured were sent to Philadelphia. Two brigades
belonging to Lord Stirling and General Adam Stephen were left on the

---

[95] Douglas S. Freeman, *George Washington, A Biography,* 4:272-73.

[96] William S. Stryker, *The Battles of Trenton and Princeton,* 14.

[97] One historian has Washington at Summerseat on December 3rd, "Washington's
head-quarters were in George Clymer's house, afterward Morrisville." Worthington
Chauncey Ford, ed., *The Writings of George Washington,* 14 vols. (New York,
1890), 5:64n. William S. Stryker, the New Jerseyan who assiduously tracked
Washington's daily whereabouts during November and December 1776, and who
frequently quotes Ford's edition of Washington's papers, is uncharacteristically silent
about December 3rd. *The Battles of Trenton and Princeton,* 15-17.

[98] Douglas S. Freeman, *George Washington: A Biography,* 4:276; William S. Stryker,
The Battles of Trenton and Princeton, 15, 310.

[99] Judge Thomas Jones, as quoted in Richard M. Ketchum, *The Winter Soldiers,* 195.

[100] The best chronological description of these two weeks is in Samuel Stelle Smith,
The Battle of Trenton, 5-7.

Jersey side "to observe the enemy's movements," General Nathanael Greene with the remaining American forces was in command at Princeton. Thus, on December 6 all the Continental Army was on the New Jersey side of the Delaware. It was during a reconnaissance to meet Lord Stirling at Princeton that Washington received news that the British Army was on the march. On December 7 the American regiments were in quick retreat. At ferries above and below the Falls the passage of General Greene, Lord Stirling and their troops continued all during the afternoon and night of December 7 and into the morning hours of December 8.[101]

As the last boatload of Americans stepped onto the Pennsylvania shore, the Hessians drummed their way into Trenton, high stepped it down to the river, and "were greeted with a shower of grapeshot from the western shore."[102]

This then was the situation on the river one half mile from Summerseat on December 7, 1776. We can imagine that one of the first boats to cross the river brought Tench Tilghman or Robert Hanson Harrison, General Washington's two aides-de-camp, to go up the hill to Summerseat to ask that the commander in chief be billeted in the Barclay residence.[103] If General Washington himself was not physically present during the night of December 7—and no source says he was—his baggage almost certainly was. The folding walnut bed and leather-covered trunks which accompanied him throughout his military campaigns would have been set up in one of the spacious downstairs rooms. The handsome mess kit would be unpacked, with

---

[101] This paragraph is based on the detailed account of Washington's retreat across the Delaware in Douglas S. Freeman, *George Washington: A Biography*, 4: 273-75; Richard K. Showman, ed., *The Papers of Nathanael Greene*, 1:366-67; and William S. Stryker, *The Battles of Trenton and Princeton*, 17-20, 27-28.

[102] William S. Stryker, *The Battles of Trenton and Princeton*, 28.

[103] Tench Tilghman, Maryland-born merchant, was a volunteer aide at that time for General Washington, having joined the commander in chief's staff a few months before. Robert Hanson Harrison was a young lawyer from Alexandria, Virginia, when he was appointed aide-de-camp to General Washington on November 5, 1775. He became his Secretary on May 16, 1776 and served in that position until he resigned in 1781. DAB; Emily Stone Whiteley, *Washington and His Aides-de-Camp* (New York, 1936), 12-14, 24,27, 136-38, 211.

Other members of Washington's staff present during this week at Summerseat were Colonel Samuel Blachley Webb of Connecticut, Colonel William Grayson of Virginia, and John Fitzgerald. John C. Fitzpatrick, editor of *The Writings of George Washington*, names the copyists of Washington's letters in his notes in volume 6:334-67.

the tin plates, cooking pots, knives, forks and various-sized bottles spread out on one of Summerseat's mahogany and walnut tables.[104]

Washington was definitely in residence at the Barclay home on the 8th, date of his first letter written to Congress from Summerseat. "Mr. Berkleys Summer Seat" now becomes the commander in chief's headquarters.[105]

It was a tense, chaotic week at Summerseat, filled with uncertainty and depressing reports: the recruitment and augmenting of the army, the whereabouts of General Lee and his divisions, the movements of the enemy, maintaining the troops in a state of readiness, the defense of Pennsylvania and the capital Philadelphia. And then there was Congress. What was Congress doing about recruiting soldiers? The plea for more troops was a constant refrain in Washington's letters to Congress that week.

As of December 8 General Washington's troops numbered between 3000 and 3500 "before [the arrival of] the Philadelphia Militia and German Battalion...." Having no intelligence of General Howe's plans and convinced that Philadelphia was his target, Washington occupied himself that week at Summerseat with defense. But defense meant more men. "Every step should be taken to collect Force not only from Pennsylvania but from the most neighbourly States...," he wrote Congress. "We may yet make a stand, if only "the Country will come to our Assistance...."[106]

Daily directives went out from Summerseat. Brigadier General William Maxwell was asked to make sure "that all the Boats and Water Craft should be secured or destroyed...."[107] General Thomas Mifflin, who was at Barclay's place on December 9, was sent to Philadelphia "to take charge of the Stores." General Israel Putnam of Connecticut, also at Summerseat those early days, was "ordered... immediately down [to Philadelphia] to superintend the Works and

---

[104] The bed, mess kit and trunks are reproduced in Richard M. Ketchum, *The World of George Washington*, 146-47. The mess kit is today in the Smithsonian Institution, Washington. The bed and trunks are at Mt. Vernon.

[105] Other headings used by Washington's secretaries during the week at Summerseat were "Falls of Delaware South Side," "Head Quarters, near Trenton," "Head Quarters, Trenton Falls," "Head Quarters, Falls of Delaware," "Trenton Falls," or simply "Bucks County."

[106] George Washington to President of Congress, Head Quarters, Trenton Falls, December 9, 1776, John C. Fitzpatrick, ed., *The Writings of George Washington*, 6:339-40.

[107] Ibid., 338.

give the necessary directions."[108]   Colonel John Cadwalader was told to have his battalions ready to march "at a Moments Warning." [109] The Pennsylvania Council of Safety was told to send the Bucks County Militia to him, not to Philadelphia.[110] Over twenty-two letters were written that week from Summerseat.[111]

---

[108] Ibid., 340.

[109] Ibid., 348.

[110] Ibid., 338.

[111] The following letters were written from Summerseat during the week of December 8-14, as far as the authors can ascertain:

December 8 -   GW to Brigadier General William Maxwell
                      GW to President of Congress
                      Colonel Henry Knox to Lucy Knox
December 9 -   GW to Pennsylvania Council of Safety
                      GW to President of Congress
December 10 -   GW to Major General Charles Lee
                      GW to President of Congress
                      William Grayson to Major John Clarke at Bristol
                      General Orders to Stirling, Mercer, Stephen de Fermoy
                      GW to Pennsylvania Council of Safety
                      GW to Lund Washington
December 11 -   GW to Colonel John Cadwalader
                      GW to Major General Charles Lee
                      GW to Brigadier General William Thompson
                      GW to President of Congress
December 12 -   GW to Governor Jonathan Trumbull
                      GW to President of Congress
                      GW to Major General William Heath
                      GW to Brigadier General Philemon Dickinson
                      GW to Sir William Howe
                      GW to Brigadier General James Ewing
                      GW to Dr. William Shippen, Jr.
                      GW to Colonel John Cadwalader
                      Anonymous [Tench Tilghman?] to Anonymous published
                      in *Independent Chronicle and the University Advertiser*
                      (Boston) of December 26, 1776 and the *Connecticut*
                      Courant and Weekly Intelligencer (Hartford) of
                      December 23,1776.
December 13 -   GW to President of Congress
December 14 -   possibly written at Summerseat before he removed to the Keith
                      residence:
                      GW to Major General Benedict Arnold
                      GW to Governor Jonathan Trumbull
                      GW to Lord Stirling

Washington kept long hours, was up and out early. Horses and grooms stood ready in the stables and in the courtyard of Summerseat. He rode out frequently to confer with his generals and to inspect the encampments of the troops, who were bivouacked up and down the Delaware. Many were on Summerseat property.[112]

By December 12 the strain on Washington and his aides was beginning to show. The Continental Army was outnumbered four to one.[113] By Friday the 13th stress was evident and taking its toll. Philadelphia had been evacuated. Congress had given Washington "full power" to direct the war, then fled to Baltimore. There still was no General Lee. Recruits were dribbling in, not nearly enough. The British were possibly attempting a river crossing at this very moment. "The crisis tightened. Every express had a new sensation to report," wrote historian Douglas S. Freeman.[114]

But Washington was showing a resolve that did not go unnoticed by his staff. "Your worthy General maintains the full possession of himself, is indefatigable by day and night," wrote General John Armstrong.[115] On the 14th, Washington had decided to move "further up the River to be with the main Body of my small Army...."[116]

The week at the Barclays had seen a resolute change in him. "He now had rested and had conquered the confusion of mind that had plagued and paralyzed him early in November."[117] Perhaps the comfortable furnishings of Summerseat and the support by the Barclay family and servants contributed to Washington's new-found strength of purpose.

---

[112] Charles Willson Peale, the artist, is one who may have pitched his tent among Summerseat's trees. "We are ordered to remove about a mile back and encamp round a field enclosed by a pine wood." Entry for December 8, 1776, "Journal by Charles Willson Peale," PMHB, 38(1914):271-72. General W. W. H. Davis, "Washington on the West Bank of the Delaware, 1776," PMHB, 4 (1880):137.

[113] "Our situation at present...is truly critical...The Enemy...amounting to about twelve thousand, are posted at Trenton, Penny Town...." George Washington to Major General William Heath, Head Quarters, near Trenton Falls, December 12, 1776, John C. Fitzpatrick, ed., *The Writings of George Washington*, 6:357. Fitzpatrick notes that the handwriting of aide-de-camp Robert Hanson Harrison shows "plainly the strain at headquarters," ibid. 6:356 n83.

[114] Douglas S. Freeman, *George Washington, A Biography*, 4:284.

[115] General John Armstrong to ?, December 10, 1776, quoted in ibid. 4:288.

[116] George Washington to President of Congress, December 13, 1776, John C. Fitzpatrick, ed., *The Writings of George Washington*, 6:364.

[117] Douglas S. Freeman, *George Washington: A Biography*, 4:288.

It looked as if the Americans would soon take the initiative. There is no evidence that planning for the Battle of Trenton took place while Washington was at Summerseat.[118] That he was planning something, though, is seen in his letter of December 14, 1776 to General Horatio Gates. "...We may yet effect an important stroke, or at least prevent General Howe from executing his plans."[119] On December 14, 1776 Washington left Summerseat to move on to other headquarters and to other battles.

Up the curving steps past two imposing marble lions, around the tables and in front of the fireplaces of Summerseat, the men who participated in the Battles of Trenton and Princeton, and later those of Brandywine, Germantown, and Monmouth, walked, wrote, sat and ate. Here these heroes of the American Revolution gathered around their commander in chief that December, 1776: William Alexander, who preferred to be called Lord Stirling; Hugh Mercer, the quiet Scotsman who was to lose his life at Princeton; Colonel Henry Knox, the chubby bookseller who later became Secretary of War; Adam Stephen, a Scottish-born surgeon and later founder of Martinsburg, West Virginia; John Armstrong, the backwoodsman from Pennsylvania's western frontier; Thomas Mifflin, the Philadelphia Quaker and future Governor of Pennsylvania; and Israel Putnam, the short, scrappy general from Connecticut.

We assume that the Barclay family was living there at the time. With residents of Philadelphia fleeing the city in panic in early December, anticipating a British takeover, we can be assured that Thomas Barclay made certain his young family was safe in their country seat.

We do know that Thomas was present. It was he who received the news from Tench Tilghman on December 26th of the victory at the Battle of Trenton, and who passed it on to those in Philadelphia. "Mr. Tilghman had come down to the Ferry & gave him [Barclay] the Acct," Robert Morris reported in a letter of December 26th to John Hancock. This was not the first report that "Genl Washington is now Master of that place" to reach Philadelphia, according to Morris, but Barclay's letter confirmed the news.[120]

---

[118] Ibid., 306 n15.

[119] George Washington to General Gates, December 14, 1776, John C. Fitzpatrick, ed., *The Writings of George Washington*, 6:372 quoted in ibid. 4:289.

[120] Robert Morris to John Hancock, Philada. Decemr. 26th. 1776, Paul H. Smith, ed., *Letters of Delegates to Congress, 1774-1789*, 24 vols. to date, (Washington, 1979-

(continued...)

History, however, was not finished with Summerseat. The mutiny in January 1781 of the Pennsylvania Line, camped across the river in a field near Trenton ferry, involved Summerseat. The story of this mutiny, so well told by Carl Van Doren in *Mutiny in January*, involved grievances on the part of unpaid, underfed, over-tired soldiers. Sir Henry Clinton, to encourage these disgruntled Americans to defect, sent two men to persuade them to come over to the British side. The Americans, however, though cold, hungry and fed up, had no intention of selling their patriotism. They held these agents captive and turned them over to a Committee of Congress, sent expressly to negotiate with the mutineers. These two spies were transported to Summerseat "under a Strong guard," where they remained while a Court of Inquiry convened at Summerseat to determine their fate. Condemned to death, the spies were hanged not far from Summerseat. The night before their execution Thomas Barclay supplied the Bible that was read to them.[121]

Members of the Court of Inquiry and the Committee of Congress present at Summerseat that January 1781 included the notable Americans Joseph Reed, President of the Supreme Council of Pennsylvania, General John Sullivan of New Hampshire, Reverend John Witherspoon, President of the College of New Jersey, Colonel Richard Butler of Pennsylvania, later known as the Indian fighter, Theodorick Bland, Congressional Delegate from Virginia, Lord Stirling again, and the key player in this drama, General Anthony Wayne, who was the commanding officer of the Pennsylvania Line at the time of the mutiny.[122]

THOMAS BARCLAY

Who was this Thomas Barclay, whose country seat offered hospitality to so many Revolutionary War heroes? Perhaps we should begin by saying who he was not. Thomas Barclay of Philadelphia and Summerseat has had the misfortune to be confused with a contemporary of the same name. The other Thomas Barclay was a

---

[120](...continued)
1996), 5:673.

[121] Carl Van Doren, *Mutiny in January: the Story of a Crisis in the Continental Army now for the first time fully told from many hiterto unknown or neglected sources both American and British* (New York, 1943),152-57.

[122] Ibid.,78-79, 108, 154-55.

New Yorker, who served the British cause until his death. It is this Barclay who has a long entry in the *Dictionary of American Biography* and it is to this British Loyalist that historian Samuel Flagg Bemis mistakenly refers in his *Guide to the Diplomatic History of the United States.*[123]

Ironically, there is not one entry in any major American biographical reference work concerning American patriot, Thomas Barclay of Philadelphia and Summerseat. This Thomas Barclay was a signer of two non-importation agreements in 1765 and 1769, elected member of every major committee during the resistance years of 1770-1775, elected to the Philadelphia Corporation in 1774, chosen a deputy delegate to the Provincial convention in 1774, voted a member of the influential Committee of Inspection and Observation, appointed to the Navy Board in 1777, contributor of £5000 to the Revolutionary War effort in 1780, appointed by Congress in 1781 the first Consul to take up his post in France, appointed in 1782 by Congress to audit the United States' public accounts in Europe, selected in 1785 by Ministers John Adams and Thomas Jefferson to negotiate the first treaty of the United States with an Arab, African and Muslim power, and named by President George Washington in 1791 as special envoy to Morocco.[124]

Summerseat's Thomas Barclay was Scots-Irish, born in Strabane, County Tyrone in Ulster in 1728. He came from a Protestant

---

[123] "Thomas Barclay," DAB, 1:596-97; Samuel Flagg Bemis and Grace Gardner Griffin, *Guide to the Diplomatic History of the United States, 1775-1921* (1935; Gloucester, 1963), 52; 158.

[124] Sources checked were: *Appleton's Cyclopaedia*, which has an entry for the English Thomas Barclay; DAB; *Dictionary of American History*, rev. ed., 8 vols., (New York, c1976-1978), which mentions two Barclays, both English; Mark Mayo Boatner, *Encyclopedia of the American Revolution*, (New York, 1966) with no Barclay entries; L. Edward Purcell, ed., *Who Was Who in the American Revolution*,(New York, 1993) with an entry on the Loyalist Thomas Barclay; and Ronald M. Gephart, *Revolutionary America: 1763-1789: a Bibliography*, 2 vols. (Washington, 1984), no Barclay entries. The electronic version of *Biography and Genealogical Master Index* lists no entries for Thomas Barclay, 1728-1793. Even the new *American National Biography*, 24 vols. (New York, 1999) overlooks him. The one American historian who has recognized Thomas Barclay as the treaty negotiator is Richard B. Morris, ed., *Encyclopedia of American History*, 6th ed., (New York, 1982), 136.

For biographical notes on Barclay see PA, 2nd ser., 1:78-79; John H. Campbell, *History of the Friendly Sons of St. Patrick and of the Hibernian Society for the Relief of Emigrants from Ireland,* (Philadelphia, 1892), 95-96; and Julian P. Boyd, ed., *The Papers of Thomas Jefferson* (hereafter PTJ), 11:493-500. For a more recent portrayal see James N. Tull and Priscilla H. Roberts, "The Forgotten Patriot," *Foreign Service Journal*, October 1994, 24-30.

mercantile and propertied family in northern Ireland, whose forebears had emigrated from western Scotland's County Ayr during the Plantation of Ulster in the seventeenth century.[125]

The exact year of Barclay's settling in Philadelphia is unknown, as is his emigration to America. He himself, writing in 1780, stated he had resided "in this country upwards of twenty years."[126] We have not found documentary evidence of his immigration in 1760 or immediately after. If he was not living in Philadelphia then, he appears at least to have passed through in 1762 with one of his father's ships out of Londonderry.[127] He may have stayed in the

---

[125] Barclay's father Robert was a merchant and ship owner in Londonderry and Strabane. He was descended from one of three Barclays who helped settle Ulster. Although Thomas's line of descent has not been completely determined, Barclay historians posit that Thomas is descended from the Perceton (Pierston) branch originating in the town of Irvine, Scotland. He is not descended from Robert Barclay, the Quaker Apologist. Charles Wright Barclay, Hubert F. Barclay, Mrs. Wilson-Fox, comps. *A History of the Barclay Family with Full Pedigree from 1066 to 1933* (London, 1933); Letter from Hubert F. Barclay to Anna Mary Moon, November 18, 1938, Anna Mary Moon Scrapbooks, 1747-1938, microfilm copy in the Tennessee State Library, Nashville; R. Burnham Moffatt, *The Barclays of New York: Who They Are and Who They are Not, - and Some Other Barclays*, 378; Leslie Barclay, comp., *History of the Scottish Barclays* (Folkestone, 1915), 84-90 ; John Strawhorn, *The History of Irvine, Royal Burgh and New Town* (Edinburgh, 1985), 45-46; James Paterson, *History of the Counties of Ayr and Wigton*, 3 vols. (Edinburgh, 1866), 3:198-201; *Irish Patent Rolls of James I. Facsimile of the Irish Record Commission's Calendar prepared prior to 1830* (Dublin, 1966), 323, 326, 339.

[126] PCC, M247, r92, i78, v4, p69.

[127] Thomas Barclay's name does not appear in the *Passenger and Immigration Lists Index*, ed. P. William Filby (Detroit, 1981) or any of the subsequent annual supplements. Although the book, *Immigrants to America Before 1750*, ed. Frederick A. Virkus (Baltimore, 1965), gives a biographical entry for Thomas Barclay (1728-1793), we have found no evidence that he emigrated prior to 1750. The earliest document we have found referring to Thomas Barclay in America is an invoice for payment of duty "on sundry Goods, Wares, Merchandize or Liquors imported to or exported from the Havana" in September 1762 in the brig *Betty*, Ralph Gill Master, signed by Barclay and dated 28 August 1767. Provincial Delegates MSS Collection, HSP, vol.1:18.

Barclay was probably supercargo on the *Betty*, a 50-ton brig in which his father and uncle were part owners. The *Betty*, registered in Philadelphia in November 1761, sailed that month for Londonderry and returned to Philadelphia in July 1762 via Liverpool. In August she was cleared for Providence and Jamaica; in September she was in Havana selling to the English, who had just captured it from the Spanish. In early December the *Pennsylvania Gazette* noted the arrival of the *Betty* from Havana. Thomas Barclay was undoubtedly on board. In early January 1763 the *Betty* was

(continued...)

colonies at that time, but if not, he returned and stayed at some point in the following two years. In August 1764, Barclay was part of the firm Barclay and Mitchell, advertising a variety of dry goods from their "linnen warehouse" in Water Street.[128]

In 1765 Barclay signed the Non-Importation Agreement on behalf of the firm Carsan, Barclay and Mitchell.[129]   When the Townshend Duties were passed, Carsan, Barclay and Mitchell again signed its name in 1768 to a protest letter, calling on English merchants to use their influence to get these duties repealed. And when that letter was ignored, in 1769 another non-importation

---

[127](...continued)
cleared for Londonderry, still with Ralph Gill as master. Throughout 1763 and 1764 under different captains she traded to Londonderry, Liverpool and Newfoundland. *Pennsylvania Journal*, November 12 & 26, 1761; July 1 & 8, August 5 & 12, 1762; January 6, 1763; February 23, August 2, 16 & 30, November 15 & 22, 1764; *Pennsylvania Gazette*, November 26, 1761; July 8, August 5 (mistakenly called the *Patty*) & 12, 1762; December 2, 1762.

References to Thomas Barclay prior to 1762 are very rare. No birth certificate or baptism record has been located. Nothing is known of his mother, his grandparents, his schooling, or the first twenty-two years of his life. The earliest document we have found is a letter to "Thos Barclay Strabane" dated November 30, 1750 in the Davey and Carsan, Letterbook, 1745-1750, LC. Having ordered twenty hogsheads of flaxseed from Philadelphia, the twenty-two-year-old young merchant was informed that "the other articles you orderd are not be be got here but at a price that wd not answer your market. old Spain is the Market to get them from." Davey and Carson Letterbook, 1745-1750, on microfilm, LC.

[128] The earliest advertisement for Barclay and Mitchell located in the Philadelphia papers was dated August 9, 1764. A search through newspapers for 1763 revealed no Barclay and Mitchell advertising.

[129] Advertisements for the firm Carsan, Barclay and Mitchell began appearing in Philadelphia newspapers in May 1765. *Pennsylvania Journal*, May 2, 9, October 24, 31, November 14, 21, 28, December 19, 26, 1765. Samuel Carsan, Barclay's uncle, advertised as an individual merchant during the years 1763 and 1764. *Pennsylvania Journal*, March 24 & 31, April 7 & 21, August 4 & 11, October 6, 13, & 20, November 10, 17 & 21, & December 1, 1763; May 3, 17, 24, & 31, August 30, September 6, 13 & 20, October 11 & 25, November 1, 8 & 29, 1764. There is no Thomas Barclay signature on the welcoming letter to Governor John Penn in November 1763 from the 168 Philadelphia merchants, although Samuel Carsan signed. *Penn Papers, Additional Miscellaneous Manuscripts*, 21 November 1763, 1:111, HSP. Printed in Thomas Willing Balch, *Willing Letters and Papers...*, 23-26. The Non-Importation Agreement is printed in J. Thomas Scharf and Thompson Westcott, *History of Philadelphia, 1609-1884*, 1:272-73, and Thomas Willing Balch, *op. cit.*, 29-40, with Carsan, Barclay and Mitchell's name on page 35. The partnership of Carsan, Barclay, and Mitchell was dissolved on May 1, 1773. *Pennsylvania Chronicle*, March 22-29, 1773, repeated in March 29-April 5 issue.

agreement was signed, with Thomas Barclay one of the signatories.[130]

Philadelphia's merchants were not a cohesive group in those years prior to Independence. They were divided by religion, by family connections, by loyalty to the Crown, and by their balance sheets. In the early 1770s many merchants were doing well by Mother England and were willing to overlook Britain's continued attempt to raise revenue in the colonies. The status quo was providing them with a good living and their ships were trading wheat, flour, and lumber to Europe and the Caribbean, bringing back molasses, rum, slaves, servants, dry goods, and manufactured goods. So when the Tea Crisis burst upon them in 1773, many merchants, "guided only by profits," did not join in the rising resistance movement.[131] Thomas Barclay never let profit margins determine his involvement in patriot politics. His bottom line was independence.

In 1770, prosperous and Presbyterian, Barclay married Mary Hoops, fourth of five daughters of Adam Hoops.[132] The early 1770s saw Barclay become involved in social and political affairs. He was an original and active member of the Friendly Sons of St. Patrick, organized in 1771, serving as its president in 1779-81. He joined the Jockey Club and began to take an increasingly active part in the political events then unfolding in Philadelphia.[133]

Barclay was a member of that merchant class in pre-Revolutionary Philadelphia to which so many historians have turned

---

[130] "From the Merchants and Traders of Philadelphia, in the Province of Pennsylvania, to the Merchants and Manufacturers of Great Britain." Undated [ca. November 1768]. MSS Relating to Non-Importation Resolutions, Philadelphia, 1765-1775, APS. Cited by Robert F. Oaks, "Philadelphia Merchants and the Origins of American Independence," *Proceedings of the American Philosophical Society*, 121 (1977, no.6):414; Robert F. Oaks, "Philadelphia Merchants and the American Revolution, 1765-1776," (PhD. diss., University of Southern California, 1970), 216.

[131] Robert F. Oaks, "Philadelphia Merchants and the American Revolution," 413.

[132] "1770 Nov. Thomas Barclay to Mary Hoops." Register of Marriages, Baptisms and Communicants kept by and for the Use of the First Presbyterian Church in the City of Philadelphia from the year 1760 to the year 1806. Marriages solemnized by Doct John Ewing, p.109. V F MI46, Manuscript in the Presbyterian Historical Society, Philadelphia.

[133] John H. Campbell, *History of the Friendly Sons of St. Patrick*, 33, 39, 45, 67-78; Register of the Jockey Club, original and a photostat, HSP. We thank independent researcher Robert E. Wright for this latter information.

their analytical minds and agile pens.[134]   When the Tea Crisis in 1773
united John Dickinson, Charles Thomson, Thomas Mifflin, and
William Bradford in epistolary resistance, Thomas Barclay was there,
supporting them, meeting with them and signing letters with them.
He was one of the group that met to decide what action to take when
the tea ship *Polly* arrived.   He was one of the twelve selected "to
persuade those Philadelphians who had been named agents by the
East India Company to resign their appointments."[135] He was among
those who met the ship and told the captain to return to England
without landing the detested tea.When a Committee of Correspondence was formed and nineteen members were selected in December
1773, Thomas Barclay was one.   He signed the letter sent to the
Boston Committee of Correspondence on December 25, 1773.[136]

Events of May 1774 spread Thomas Barclay's name beyond
Pennsylvania into the other colonies.   Great Britain had upped the
ante when it announced the closing of the port of Boston on June 1st,
1774, in retaliation for the Boston Tea Party.   This was the event
which brought Paul Revere galloping into Philadelphia on May 19th.
A meeting was called on the 20th and on the 21st "that patriotic
document" calling for a convention of all the colonies was drafted
and signed by nineteen prominent citizens, of whom Thomas Barclay
was one, and given to Paul Revere to carry back to Boston.   This

---

[134] Arthur M. Schlesinger, *Colonial Merchants and the American Revolution, 1763-
1776* (New York, 1968); Carl Bridenbaugh, *Cities in Revolt: Urban Life in America,
1743-1776* ; Arthur Jensen, *Maritime Commerce in Colonial Philadelphia*; Robert
F. Oaks, "Philadelphia Merchants and the Origins of American Independence,"
Proceedings of the APS 121 (1977, no.6), Gary B. Nash, *The Urban Crucible: Social
Change, Political Consciousness, and the Origins of the American Revolution;*
Richard A. Ryerson, *The Revolution is Now Begun: The Radical Committees of
Philadelphia, 1765-1776* (Philadelphia, 1978) and Thomas M. Doerflinger, *A
Vigorous Spirit of Enterprise: Merchants and Economic Development in
Revolutionary Philadelphia* .

[135] Richard A. Ryerson, *The Revolution is Now Begun*, 34-37, 80 (table 4); "How
the Landing of Tea was Opposed in Philadelphia by Colonel William Bradford and
Others in 1773," PMHB, 15 (1891, no.4): 385-93;   Frank M. Etting, *The
Philadelphia Tea Party of 1773. A Chapter from the History of the Old State House*
(Philadelphia, December 17th, 1873); Benjamin Woods Labaree, *The Boston Tea
Party* (Boston, 1964), 97-102.

[136] "To the Committee at Boston from the Committee of Philadelphia," December 25,
1773, New York Public Library, Bancroft Collection, Boston Committee of
Correspondence - Pennsylvania. A copy is also in the New York Historical Society,
Manuscript Department.

letter was published throughout the colonies.[137]

The Committee that laid the groundwork for the first Provincial Convention of Pennsylvania was alternately called the Provincial Committee, Committee of Forty-Three, or Committee of Correspondence. Thomas Barclay was an elected member.[138] When this Convention convened in Carpenter's Hall on July 4, 1774, Thomas Barclay was selected one of the deputies. He was also present at the Convention held at Philadelphia on July 15, 1774.[139] Barclay was elected to the Philadelphia Corporation, as the city common council was then called. By 1774, however, it was on the wane and Barclay is listed as having attended only two meetings. By spring 1776 the Corporation was out of existence.[140]

A sign of Barclay's rising prominence was his dinner guest on October 14, 1774. George Washington, in town for the Continental Congress, noted in his diary "Dined at Mr. Thos. Barclay's...."[141]

As events accelerated, so did Thomas Barclay's involvement. In 1775 he was one of the delegates from the city of Philadelphia to the Pennsylvania Provincial Convention held on January 23, 1775.[142] On February 16, 1775 as a member of the Committee of Correspondence of Philadelphia, he signed the letter to the Committee of Correspondence of New York, assuring them "...that the inhabitants of

---

[137] Richard A. Ryerson, *The Revolution is Now Begun*, 40-45, 81 (table 5); PA, 2nd ser., 1:82; Peter Force, *American Archives*, 4th ser., 340-41; *Virginia Gazette*, June 23, 1774; *Pennsylvania Gazette*, June 8, 1774; *Calendar of Virginia State Papers*, 8:45, 55; "Biographical Sketch of Joseph Fox," PMHB, 32 (1908, no.2): 189, and J. Thomas Scharf and Thompson Westcott, *History of Philadelphia, 1609-1884*, 1:289.

[138] Richard A. Ryerson, *The Revolution is Now Begun*, 84 (table 6); for a discussion of the committee's evolution and actions, see 52-57. The committee members' names are printed in several places: Rivington's *New York Gazetteer*, June 22, 1774; *Pennsylvania Journal*, June 22, 1774; J. Thomas Scharf and Thompson Westcott, *History of Philadelphia, 1609-1884*, 1:290.

[139] PA, 2nd ser., 3:590: "Officers of the State of Pennsylvania in the Revolution and Under the Constitution of 1776;" ibid., 3: 473:" Minutes of the Provincial Deputies"; *Carpenters' Hall and its Historic Memories* (Philadelphia, 1876), 6-7.

[140] PA, 2nd ser., 9:752; Judith M. Diamondstone, "The Philadelphia Corporation, 1701-1776," (PhD diss. University of Pennsylvania, 1969), 381-82; *Minutes of the Common Council of the City of Philadelphia, 1704-1776* (Philadelphia, 1847), 799, 801.

[141] Donald Jackson, ed., *The Diaries of George Washington*, 6 vols.(Charlottesville, 1976-1979), 3:285-86.

[142] PA, 2nd ser., 3:549, 591.

Pennsylvania continue immoveably firm to the cause of liberty...."[143]

In early 1777 Thomas Barclay was appointed to the Navy Board,[144] and soon after he took the oath of allegiance to the state of Pennsylvania. In July he offered "a small Cargo of Salt in Tom's River, in New Jersey..." to sell to the Supreme Executive Council of Pennsylvania "for the use of the People of this State."[145] In September General Howe marched into Philadelphia and for the next nine months British troops occupied the city. The Barclay family was safely ensconced at Summerseat, thirty miles away.[146]

As the war effort intensified, Barclay was one of several prominent Philadelphians who contributed £5000 to the organization of the Pennsylvania Bank, established to raise funds to supply the Continental Army. Along with Samuel Meredith he also helped obtain and forward wagons of flour to Washington's troops at Trenton.[147]

---

[143] Committee of Correspondence of Philadelphia to the Committee of Correspondence of New-York, February 16, 1775. Signed by John Cadwallader, Thomas Barclay, Samuel Meredith, James Mease, Joseph Read, Thomas Mifflin, George Clymer, Jonathan B. Smith, John Nixon. Peter Force, ed. *American Archives*, 4th ser., 1243.

[144] PA, 2nd ser. (1896 repr. ed.), 1: 78; III:621; Colonial Records (Minutes of the Supreme Council of Pennsylvania), 9:127.

[145] PA, 2nd ser., 3:7; Colonial Records, 9:249.

[146] The one letter located written by Thomas Barclay from Summerseat during the British occupation of Philadelphia is dated November 1st, 1777. It deals with family matters & alludes only briefly to the difficult times. "I had some thoughts of Embarquing for Europe, but cannot think of leaving my family at the present juncture & I have therefore at present laid aside all thoughts of that voyage." Writing to his brother-in-law in Albemarle County, Virginia, Barclay asked him about "a place for sale in Virginia. It is call'd Scotchtown and belongs to Mr. Henry...Give me as exact a discription [sic] as your memory will permit...write me something of the quality of the land - If it was offerd on reasonable terms, I believe I should think of purchasing especialy if the present situation of affairs continue [sic]." Thomas Barclay to Thomas Walker, Jr., Summerseat, 1 November 1777, Thomas Walker Papers in the William Cabell Rives Papers, Reel 2, Container 162, LC.

[147] Lawrence Lewis, Jr., *A History of the Bank of North America: The First Bank Chartered in the United States* (Philadelphia, 1882), 19; A. J. McClurkin, "Summary of the Bank of North America Records," PMHB, 64 (January 1940): 90; Samuel Meredith and Thomas Barclay to General George Washington, Trenton, June 24, July 1, and August 27, 1780; George Washington to Meredith and Barclay, June 27 and July 24, 1780, The Papers of George Washington, Manuscript Division, LC; and William Nelson, ed., *Documents Relating to the Revolutionary History of the State*

(continued...)

Meanwhile in France American Minister Benjamin Franklin had been pleading for Congress to send him a consul.[148] Finally acceding to his request Congress named William Palfrey, a Massachusetts merchant and a paymaster general to the Continental Army, as our first consul. Palfrey set sail in December 1780 from Philadelphia on board the *Shellelagh*, but neither was ever heard from again.[149] Some months later Congress appointed Thomas Barclay in his place. His appointment as Consul "by the United States in Congress assembled" was signed by Thomas McKean, President of the Continental Congress, on October 5, 1781.[150]

The next day the Barclay family embarked on board the *St. James*, Thomas Truxtun captain, for Lorient, France. They almost didn't make it. Within hours of sailing, the *St. James* was attacked by a New York Tory privateer, which carried on a bloody battle for "three glasses" and came away the loser. Although three crewmen and a passenger were killed and others wounded in the battle, the damaged *St. James* continued on its maiden voyage to France.[151]

---

[147](...continued)
of New Jersey, Extracts from American Newspapers relating to New Jersey, Nov. 1, 1779-Sept. 30,1780 (Trenton, 1914), 4:463.

[148] "The little authority we have here to govern our armed ships and the inconvenience of distance from the ports occasion abundance of irregularities in the conduct of both men and officers. I hope, therefore, that no more of those vessels will be sent hither....They give me infinite trouble...I have often mentioned the appointment of a consul or consuls...," Franklin to the President of Congress, Passy, August 9, 1780, *The Revolutionary Diplomatic Correspondence of the United States*, 4:22; Jonathan R. Dull, "Franklin the Diplomat: the French Mission," *Transactions of the American Philosophical Society*, 72, Pt. 1 (1982):66.

[149] A black marble plaque at the Department of State in Washington is dedicated to American diplomatic and consular officers who "lost their lives under heroic or tragic circumstances." "William Palfrey, Lost at Sea, 1780" heads the list.

[150] Barclay was named vice consul on July 10 1781, JCC, 20:735-37. When it became certain that Palfrey was lost, Barclay petitioned Congress to be named consul. This was granted on October 5, 1781. Ibid. 21:1036. A copy of Barclay's commission is in the Benjamin Franklin Papers, University of Pennsylvania Library.

[151] The battle between the *Goodrich* and *St. James* was reported in the *Freeman's Journal or, The North-American Intelligencer*, October 24, 1781 and *Pennsylvania Packet, or the General Advertiser*, October 23, 1781, copying the despatch from Rivington's New York *Royal Gazette* of October 13th. It makes lively reading. "On Wednesday morning last, after chasing all the preceding night he [Captain Buchanan of the *Goodrich*] came up with, off Cape Henlopen, the rebel ship *St. James* of 28 guns...bound from Philadelphia to Port l'Orient, having on board six hundred
(continued...)

[151](...continued)
hogsheads of tobacco. - He brought her to action within pistol shot, and continued to engage her...for two glasses; an unfortunate shot which carried away his tiller ropes and block early in the action, gave the enemy an opportunity of disabling his rigging so much that after nearly silencing our fire, she made sail and effected her escape. The *Goodrich* having her main mast badly wounded in three places, and her standing and running rigging much shattered, could not set sufficient sail to come up with her...."

Upon arrival in Lorient Captain Truxtun of the *St. James* sent this report back to Philadelphia: "I Sailed the 9th. ulto. from Cape Henlopen with the wind at about West, a Good breeze and pleasant weather. Three hours after I left the Capes two Sail was discovered from the fore top-mast head, just before the weather beam...which bore down upon us. I Edged away about two points. The wind at this time had got to the S S W, and crowded all the Sail I could sett. At twelve at night I immagined we gained on her but the wind falling light at about 4 in the morning she gained on us by taking the breeze first. Knowing the ship was too much by the head I Ordered the anchors Cut from the bows and Every man to set down Aft on the quarter deck. Notwithstanding this I found she came up with the breeze fast. I then ordered all hands to quarters and got Every thing in as Good order as was possible for a new Ship only out a few hours. At 6 a.m. being day-light, I saw she was a Copper bottom Kings Ship mounting 24 or 26 Guns...She was then about a mile distance. Finding it impossible to avoid an action with her as their was Every appearance of the weather being Calm, I hawled up my Courses & down Jib & Stay-sails and hove too for her. She came up along side of me and hoisted the blue English Ensign at Mizzen Peak. As soon as I saw her Collours going up I ordered the whole broad-side fired into her. She immediately Returned it. This brought on a severe action for three Glasses in the Course of which I raked her thrice, brought down her fore yard and did her such damage that from my braces, etc. being all shot away She fell a-thwart my hawse at distance of twenty yards and never fired a shott. I then bore away to Refit. She hawled her wind and went off standing towards Sandy Hook. We gave her three Cheers which she did not Return...." Thomas Truxtun to Mesrs. A. & J. Caldwell & Others, Owners of Ship *St. James*, L'Orient 17th Nov. 1781, Record Group 45, Naval Records Collection of the Office of Naval Records & Library, Area File 4, National Archives (hereafter NA). One of the wounded passengers, writing later in life, did not expect to recover from the "musquet Ball" in his shoulder. "A Philadelphia Merchant in 1768-1791," PMHB, 19 (1895):397-402.

We have no reason to believe that the *St. James* was targeted by the British for the sole purpose of capturing the American consul, as some writers have stated. Charles W. Goldsborough, *The United States Naval Chronicle*,(Washington, 1824), 1:28, and Edgar S. Maclay, *A History of American Privateers* (New York, 1899), 87. The "Kings ship" *Goodrich* was owned by the "infamous Goodrich" of the Virginia Tory family, whose privateers caused much havoc to the colonialists. Gardner W. Allen, *A Naval History of the American Revolution*, 2 vols. (1913; New York, 1962),1:139; 2: 398, 569; Lorenzo Sabine, *Biographical Sketches of Loyalists of the American Revolution*, 2 vols. (1864; Port Washington, NY, 1966), 1:480-81, and Gregory Palmer, *Biographical Sketches of Loyalists of the American Revolution*, rev. ed. of Sabine's work cited above, (Westport, 1984), 324. All American ships were fair game during the Revolution, no matter who or what was on board. The 600

(continued...)

During Thomas Barclay's six years as our consular representative to France—he was promoted to Consul General by Congress in January 1783—he was given responsibilities far beyond those of a consul today. Not only was he to "receive and forward all supplies to be obtained in that kingdom [France] for the use of the United States," but Barclay was also asked "to assist in directing our naval affairs," to "regularly transmit to us accounts of the civil and military constitutions of the place...of its advantages for commerce with the world in general, and especially with these United States."[152] How well he succeeded can be seen in the lengthy reports he sent back to Robert R. Livingston, Secretary of Foreign Affairs, and to Congress.[153]

---

[151](...continued)
hogsheads of tobacco appeared to be more of a lure than the American consul. After all, money from its sale could be divvied up among the crew.

[152] JCC, 20:736.

[153] Barclay's fifteen official despatches to Secretary Livingston between 7 March 1782 and 14 November 1783 are found in the PCC, Record Group 360 on microfilm M247, r119, i91, v1, with the exception of despatch nos. 3 and 5, which have not been located, and despatch #13. This latter despatch, dated 14 September 1783, is in M247, r150, i137,v4, p309 and is printed unnumbered in *The Diplomatic Correspondence of the United States of America from the signing of the Definitive Treaty of Peace, 10th September 1783, to the Adoption of the Constitution, March 4, 1789* (Washington, 1833), 6 vols., 1:489-90. A copy of despatch #14 dated 20 October 1783 is also in the Benjamin Franklin Papers in the APS Library. Livingston's official letters to Barclay are dated 28 November 1781 to 26 November 1782 and are found in the PCC, M247, r105,i79, v1. The last despatch dated 26 November 1782 is printed unnumbered in Wharton, *Revolutionary Diplomatic Correspondence of the United States*, 6:82. Copies also are in the Robert R. Livingston Papers, New York Historical Society.

As a public official in Europe Barclay served three bosses. As Consul and later Consul General his immediate superior in Paris was Benjamin Franklin (and from 1784 Thomas Jefferson); in Congress it was the Secretary of Foreign Affairs (from October 20, 1781, Robert R. Livingston; from December 1784, John Jay). As Commissioner of Public Accounts, Barclay reported to Robert Morris, Superintendent of Finance.

For references to Thomas Barclay and occasional letters to him by Franklin, see the Benjamin Franklin Letterbook in LC, especially those letters dated 26 November 1781, 6 December 1781,17 December 1781, 18 January 1782, 4 February 1782, 12 February 1782, 22 February 1782, and 4 March 1782.

Other references to Barclay can be found in *The Diplomatic Correspondence of the United States*, 1:459-504, on M247, r150 and in Francis Wharton, ed., *Revolutionary Diplomatic Correspondence of the United States* , 5:54,163,513-14,796; 6:82, 114-19;380;736-37,786-87, 800, and under "Barclay" in the index,

(continued...)

The onerous task of trying to settle all public accounts of the United States in Europe was given to Barclay by Congress on November 18, 1782. This time-consuming assignment took him to the French Atlantic seaports, wherever agents handled American shipping, and to London and Brussels to interrogate Silas Deane and to try to sort out his accounts. Working on the complex and confusing papers of Pierre Caron de Beaumarchais, the bon vivant playwright-cum secret agent-cum shipping supplier, delayed the departure of Barclay's Morocco mission.[154]

He also served as agent to purchase arms for the state of Virginia,[155] and in 1785 he was named special envoy to Morocco to negotiate a treaty with Sultan Sidi Muhammad ibn Abdallah. Departing Paris in January 1786 with David S. Franks as his secretary, Barclay traveled by post chaise down the coast of France, across Spain to Cadiz, where they took ship to Mogador (today's Essaouira), Morocco. In Madrid they had been received by King Charles III, who facilitated their visit to Morocco by sending a letter of introduction to the Sultan. Traveling with two French servants, a Spanish-English dictionary, a copy of Don Quixote, and dozens of carefully-selected gifts for the Sultan and his courtiers—including two spectacular clocks—Barclay and Franks reached Marrakech in June, had two audiences with the Sultan Sidi Muhammad, and signed a treaty of Peace and Friendship on June 26. This treaty, which, to the surprise of many, required the United States to pay no annual tribute, was ratified by Congress and remained in effect for fifty years. Although a new treaty was signed in 1837, all the articles negotiated by Barclay in 1786, with one exception, were maintained in the new treaty. Barclay's intelligence reports from Morocco, models of perspicacity and clarity, have been published in *The Papers of Thomas*

---

[153](...continued)
849.

[154] Eight pages of detailed instructions drafted by Congress for Barclay are given in John Catanzariti et al, eds., *The Papers of Robert Morris*, 7:168-75, and in Wharton, *Revolutionary Diplomatic Correspondence of the United States*, 6:115-19. See also E. James Ferguson, *The Power of the Purse* (Chapel Hill, 1961), 195-98, and Thomas Jefferson to John Adams, Paris December 11, 1785, PTJ, 9:91.

[155] William P. Palmer and H. W. Flournoy, eds., *Calendar of Virginia State Papers and Other Manuscripts...Preserved in the Capitol at Richmond*, 11 vols (Richmond, 1875-1893), 3: 390; William T. Hutchinson and William M.E. Rachal, eds., *Papers of James Madison*, 6:411-13.

Jefferson.[156]

Once the Barclays left Summerseat in 1781 for France, they never again took up residence in Bucks County. By the time Thomas Barclay had returned to Philadelphia in October 1787, he was financially embarrassed, in debt to creditors in France, England, and Pennsylvania, and a fugitive from a French debtor's prison.[157] Consuls in those days and for many years thereafter were expected to earn most of their livelihood by engaging in trade. Barclay's time-consuming duties in the service of his country left him too little time to devote to his own finances. He was a careful man and an honest one—"indeed he is incapable of doing anything not strictly honourable," Thomas Jefferson wrote in 1787. But bad luck—his business partner in France died suddenly, leaving large debts—and the increasingly depressed world economy in the 1780s plagued him for the rest of his life. Returning to Philadelphia, Barclay hoped to straighten out his finances, pay off his debts, and return to France to rejoin his family. However, by early 1788, he wrote Thomas Jefferson, our Minister to France, to ask that his family return to join him in Philadelphia. Mary Barclay and the four children—a third daughter had been born in Auteuil in March 1784—sailed from Bordeaux in August on board the *MISSOURI*, Captain Elias Boys master, arriving in Philadelphia on October 5, 1788. Mary Hoops Barclay had last seen her husband in January 1786.

---

[156] PTJ, 10:334-48; 389-92; 418-27. Barclay's letters from 1782-1788 and extensive accounts for the Morocco mission can be found in PCC, M247, r119, i91, v1:1-325, and v2:326-436. The treaty is printed in Charles I. Bevans, comp., *Treaties and Other International Agreements of the United States of America, 1776-1949* (Washington, 1972), 9:1278-1285. For other sources of the printed treaty see Igor I. Kavass and Mark A. Michael, comps., *United States Treaties and Other International Agreements Cumulative Index 1776-1949*, 4 vols (Buffalo, 1975), vol.3. See also James N. Tull and Priscilla H. Roberts, "The Forgotten Patriot," *Foreign Service Journal*, October 1994, 24-30; Priscilla H. Roberts and James N. Tull, "Emissary to Barbary," *Aramco World*, September/October 1998, 49(no. 5), 28-35; and Priscilla H. Roberts and James N. Tull, "Moroccan Sultan Sidi Muhammad Ibn Abdallah's Diplomatic Initiatives Toward the United States, 1777-1786," *Proceedings of the American Philosophical Society*, 143 (no. 2), June 1999, 233-65.

[157] Thomas Barclay to Thomas Jefferson, Bordeaux June 12, 1787; Jefferson to John Jay, Paris June 21, 1787 with extensive editorial notes on Barclay's arrest; Thomas Barclay to Thomas Jefferson, Bordeaux June 29, 1787; Thomas Barclay to Thomas Jefferson, ca July 3, 1787; John Bondfield to Thomas Jefferson, Bordeaux July 3, 1787, PTJ, 11: 466-67; 477-79; 491-500; 504-06; 534-38; 538-39; Ibid. 13:253; Ibid. 15:45,109.

Barclay mortgaged Summerseat in October 1787.[158]   He petitioned Congress for salary that had never been paid during the years serving his country abroad. The request was periodically referred to committee and it was not acted upon until long after his death.[159] He declared bankruptcy and Summerseat was sold to his creditors in 1791.[160]

Thomas Barclay's finances are a tangled affair. It is difficult to sort them out because no financial documents or ledgers have yet been located. He evidently did manage to clear his name, as in 1791 he was once again called to the service of his country. His friend Thomas Jefferson persuaded Washington to offer Barclay a special mission to Morocco to renegotiate the treaty with the new sultan.

---

[158] Mortgage Deed from Thomas Barclay to Eddowes, Petrie and Ellis, dated October 19, 1787, recorded April 14, 1788, Bucks County Deed Book 24, 203-06.

[159] The extensive documentation on Mary Barclay's claim is in the *American State Papers*, 38 vols. (Washington, 1832-1861), Class 9. Claims, 347-54, dated January 8, 1808. Discussion of the claim by the House and Senate and its approval on April 18, 1808 can be found in *Debates and Proceedings in the Congress of the United States; with an Appendix Containing Important State Papers and Public Documents...Tenth Congress-First Session* (spine title: *Annals of Congress*) (Washington, 1852), 359-60, and *United States Statutes At Large, 1789-1845* (Boston, 1848), 6:72, chap.45. $14,190.78 was authorized to be paid to Thomas Barclay's "legal representatives" on August 1, 1808, and on August 2nd warrant no. 363 was issued for that amount "in favor of Robt. Barclay & Peyton Harrison [illegible, abbreviation for Attorneys?] Mary Barclay [illegible, abbreviation for Administrix?] of Thomas Barclay dec'd...," Record Group 217 (Accounting Officers of the Department of Treasury), Entry 347, Settled Accounts of the First Auditor, Account #20677, M235, Miscellaneous Accounts of the First Auditor (Formerly The Auditor) of the Treasury Department, September 6, 1790-1840, on Roll 64, frames 316-318, NA; United States, Department of the Treasury, *An Account of the Receipts and Expenditures of the United States for the Year 1808.* (City of Washington, 1808), 57; and Entry 33, p. 12, Series Daybooks, Sept. 13, 1789-Sept. 29, 1894. 9.1M, 30 ft., 110 vols, volume for the year 1808. We thank Mary Frances Morrow, Old Military and Civil Records, and Wayne T. De Cesar, Archivist, Civilian Records, both of the Textual Archives Services Division, NA for these citations. Barclay's creditors received their dividend soon after, when half the awarded amount was sent to Philadelphia by Robert Barclay. *Aurora General Advertiser* (Philadelphia), August 23, 1808; Letter of John Barclay to Robert Barclay, September 1, 1808, Dr. James Barclay Donaldson Bequest, Bethany College Archives, Bethany, WV.

[160] Thomas Barclay to Thomas Jefferson, Philadelphia, April 19, 1791, PTJ, 20:239; Deed from Robert Ralston, Assignee for Thomas Barclay, a Bankrupt, to Blair McClenachan for lands in the Northern Liberties, September 9, 1791, Deeds-4th floor, HSP; Deed of Sale of Summerseat between John Ashley, attorney for Barclay's creditors, and Robert Morris, November 28, 1791, Bucks County Box, HSP; and PA, 6th ser., 12:240-41.

Barclay accepted. Mary Hoops Barclay and the children went to Virginia to live with her sister Sarah Syme, and he sailed for Oporto, Portugal in August 1791 to launch his mission to Morocco.[161]

The Moroccan Sultan had died in April 1790 and his death was followed by over three years of internecine fighting among his four sons and their followers. There was no one in Morocco with whom a foreign envoy could negotiate. The anarchy in Morocco left Barclay biding his time in Lisbon, Gibraltar and Cadiz, whence he periodically sent dispatches to Jefferson. Before a new sultan had been proclaimed, Barclay fell ill and died on January 19, 1793. He was buried in St. George's Anglican Church cemetery in Lisbon, in a grave that no longer exists, or at least, is not marked.[162]

SUMMERSEAT THE HOUSE

The lands that became Summerseat were purchased by Adam Hoops in 1764, 1765, and 1766.[163] These three parcels of land,

---

[161] Thomas Barclay to TJ, Philadelphia March 12, 1791; PTJ, 19:535; Official Instructions for Thomas Barclay, Philadelphia May 13, 1791; Confidential Instructions for Thomas Barclay, May 13, 1791; Ibid. 20:397-401. Washington's letter to the Emperor of Morocco of March 31, 1791, cited in Julian P. Boyd's editorial note on p. 399, has been returned from Australia and is now in the Bethany College Archives, Bethany, West Virginia.

[162] David Humphreys to the Secretary of State, Lisbon January 23, 1793, "Mr. Barclay, Consul for Morocco, who arrived here from Cadiz on Tuesday last, died on Saturday. His sudden death is supposed to have been occasioned by an inflamation [sic] of the lungs...." Diplomatic Despatches from United States Ministers to Portugal, M43, r2, v3, letter no. 64, NA. His burial is noted in the manuscript register, "Marriages, Baptisms and Burials, 1721 to 1807," belonging to St. George's Church, Lisbon, under date of January 21, 1793: "Thomas Barclay Esqre Consul from the United States to Morocco aged 65." The burial ground lost some of its land in the 1940s, when the city of Lisbon needed to widen a street. Thirty-five graves were dug up and removed, but no records exist showing that one was Thomas Barclay's grave. John D. Hampton, *History of the Lisbon Chaplaincy*, 2nd ed. with revisions by Reverend E.N. Staines (Lisbon, 1989), 58-61. We acknowledge the gracious help of Mrs. Joan de Moura of Lisbon during our visit there.

On one of the cemetery walls is a large plaque erected by a Barclay descendant in 1971. This plaque wrongly informs visitors that Thomas Barclay was killed in a duel.

[163] Deed of Indenture between Josiah Wood and wife and Adam Hoops dated 14 August 1764 for seventy acres plus a 30-acre island, Bucks County Deed Book 15, 12-15; Deed of Indenture between William Morris and wife and Adam Hoops dated 3 August 1765 for three acres, Bucks County Deed Book 11, 661-62; Deed of Indenture

(continued...)

totaling 277 acres, had been part of a larger tract granted to John Wood in 1679 by Sir Edmond Andros, Governor of New York (whose territory then encompassed Pennsylvania). Andros had purchased "All that Tract of Land lying being on the Westside of Delaware River... about Eight or Nine Miles below the Falls, & as far abve the sd Falls as the other is & below them..." from the Indian sachems in 1675.[164] Most of it had remained in the Wood family ever since, passing to his son Joseph, then to grandsons Jabus (or Jabes), Josiah, and Benjamin, and finally to great grandsons Benjamin and Josiah.[165]

We do not know exactly when Adam Hoops moved to Bucks County or when Summerseat was built. [166] We do know that in 1772 Summerseat was described as a "large new and well finished brick house" and we understand from historians and architectural preservationists that construction of country seats similar in size to Summerseat took from three to five years. [167] This suggests that

---

[163](...continued)
between Benjamin Wood and wife and Adam Hoops dated 2 December 1766 for 174 acres, Bucks County Deed Book 15,15-18. See also the Mortgage Indenture between Benjamin Wood and Adam Hoops dated 20 March 1765, Bucks County Deed Book 11, 336-37.

[164] "Minute Book 'G'," PA, 2nd ser., 19:309; Ibid., 2nd ser., 5:703-05. The John Wood tract of land fronting the Delaware River is clearly shown on the Thomas Holme map of Pennsylvania c1685.

[165] John Wood Will no. 133 of 1692; Jabus Wood Will no. 1124 of 1763; Josiah Wood Will no. 1151 of 1764, all in Bucks County Register of Wills, Doylestown; Arnold Wood, *John Wood of Attercliffe, Yorkshire, England and Falls, Bucks County, Pennsylvania and His Descendants in the United States* (New York, 1903). We thank Betty Huber for this latter reference.

[166] Efforts were made in 1986 and 1994 to learn the origins of Summerseat. Barbara Liggett, consulting archeologist for the Bucks County Conservancy (today's Heritage Conservancy), gave the mid-1760's as "the best date." *Report on Investigations at Summerseat, Morrisville. For the Bucks County Conservancy, 15 July, 1986*, 14. Martin Jay Rosenblum, R.A. & Associates reported that "the house can be comfortably dated 1766-1771," *Historic Structure Report: Summerseat, Hillcrest and Legion Avenues, Morrisville, Pennsylvania* (Philadelphia, July 1994), 3. Copies of these xerographic reports are at the Historic Morrisville Society (hereafter HMS). The historical background in the Liggett report is replete with errors and should be passed over.

[167] Margaret B. Tinkcom, "Cliveden: The Building of a Philadelphia Countryseat, 1763-1767," PMHB, 88 (January 1964), 3-36; Mark Reinberger, "The Evolution of Woodford, an Eighteenth-Century 'Retirement'," PMHB, 121 (January/April 1997),
(continued...)

construction would have had to begin in the period 1767-1769; it could not have been earlier because the property was purchased only in December 1766. It is unlikely work could have begun before the spring of 1767. It would probably not have been completed before 1770, or even later. Hoops died at Summerseat in June of 1771.[168]

The house sat on a promontory overlooking a tree-lined carriageway sloping down to the Delaware river. No buildings obstructed its view for over a half mile. There was a private boat landing, close to the "Great Road" from Philadelphia to Trenton. Outbuildings included a stone kitchen just behind the main house, a cobblestone courtyard, stables, coach house, a large stone barn, a blacksmith shop, servants' quarters, two dwelling houses, in one of which was a store, and "other offices erected on the premises."[169]

Contiguous to the Summerseat property Adam Hoops owned twenty acres on which he had built "a compleat merchant mill, 60 x 54 feet, accommodated with one pair of burr, one pair of Cologne, and one pair of country stones, with scales and weights, a rolling screen, boulting works and hoisting geers all going by water." On this mill property were a two-story frame dwelling house, a kitchen, stone stable and barn, a blacksmith's shop, and a landing for boats to "come into the dam, and deliver their grain almost at the mill door."[170] The Hoops Mill was a landmark in the area, and in 1776 it figured in General Washington's troop deployment plans.[171] Adam Hoops's Morrisville property appears to be the earliest industrial development in Falls Township, a community of skilled craftsmen, millers and farmers working in a prime location where "a town at this

---

[167](...continued)
48; and Rosenblum R. A. & Associates, *Historic Structure Report: Summerseat*, 3.

[168] From both the date line and the content of the few surviving Hoops letters from 1767-1771, we know that he spent time at Summerseat, as well as in Philadelphia. The Summerseat letters were written in summer months and he died there in June; it may have been, as the name suggests, a summer home. The property included a house when he purchased it from Benjamin Wood in 1766 (Wood's father had died there in 1759 or 1760); this would have provided a place for him to stay while the house to be described in 1772 as "large new and well finished brick house" was being built.

[169] *Pennsylvania Gazette*, April 30, 1772.

[170] Ibid.

[171] Samuel Stelle Smith, *The Battle of Trenton*, 7.

place is wished for."[172]

Looking at this Georgian manor house today sitting in the midst of pre-World War II bungalows and next door to a school parking lot, it is difficult to imagine the Summerseat estate that was the home of the Hoops and Barclay families and, briefly, the residence of

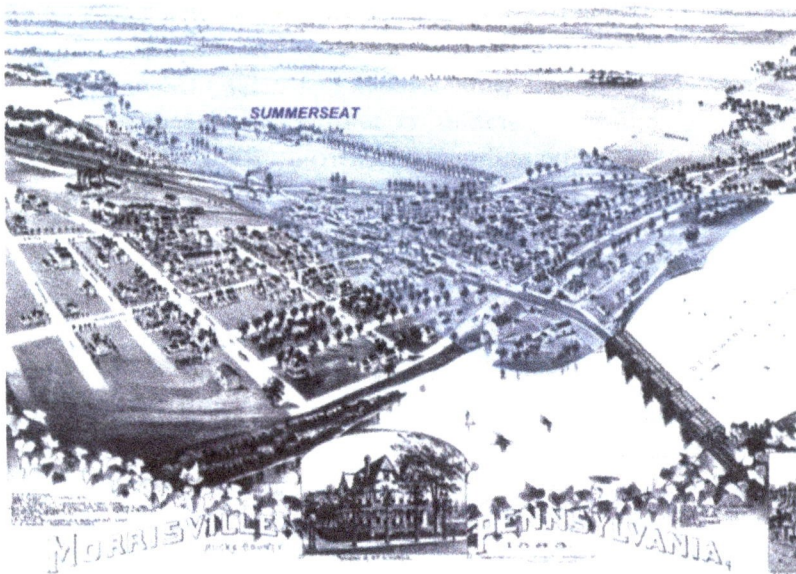

Map 2. Detail of 1893 map of Morrisville showing the Summerseat property (shaded blue), with the manor house upper center at the end of the long lane of tall cedars. Outbuildings can be seen among the trees. When Adam Hoops owned the Summerseat property it extended from beyond the top of the map down to the river. T. M. Fowler. *Morrisville, Pennsylvania* [1893]. Panoramic Map #809. Original in the collection of the Geography and Map Division, Library of Congress.

George Washington. The house is all that remains of the estate that Adam Hoops put together, which at his death included 85 acres of crop land, 40 acres cleared meadow, 95 acres of woods, and two orchards.

But, what a house. Even after 230 years, vandalized, mutilated, patched up, added to, haphazardly repaired, occasionally renovated, and subsequently restored, Summerseat still evokes its strength of

---

[172] *Pennsylvania Gazette*, April 30, 1772.

character. That was evident in 1905, when William W. H. Davis called it "the best sample of a colonial residence in the county."[173] It was evident in 1994, when architect Peter Andrew Copp noted it "must have been among the better houses in Colonial America."[174]

Summerseat reflects its colonial origins in its rectangular plan, two-and-a-half story height, its quality exterior stonework and the placement of the windows across the front, thirteen in this case. The interior of Summerseat hints at its former grandeur. The floors of yellow pine, the geometric design of the original plaster ceiling remaining in one room, the tabernacle frames over fireplace mantels, the polished wood balustrade curving up two and one half stories show details of what must have been an architecturally significant Bucks County dwelling in the eighteenth century.

The two first floor front rooms, flanking a central hallway extending from front to back, were among the best in the house, along with the ballroom on the second floor. Although the original mantels in these rooms have not survived, "the remaining historic building fabric strongly suggests that these three rooms were originally even more richly appointed" than the other first and second floor rooms.

> Few surviving Colonial houses have such richly detailed lesser rank rooms... the first floor central hall, the best parlour and the ballroom have, or had, decorative plaster ceilings a relatively uncommon feature in the Philadelphia region. The first and second floor southwestern rooms have, or had, tabernacle frames over their fireplace mantel shelves. This is quite remarkable since these are not even the best rooms in the manor house.[175]

According to architect Peter Andrew Copp, Summerseat had "architectural flourishes that characterize homes such as Mount Pleasant, Cliveden, Port Royal and the townhouses of Samuel Powel and John Cadwalader...Enough historic building fabric, either original or early, survives to tell the story of this significant house."[176]

---

[173] William W. H. Davis, *History of Bucks County Pennsylvania* (2nd ed., 1905), 2:168.

[174] Rosenblum R.A. & Associates, *Historic Structure Report: Summerseat*, 14.

[175] Ibid., 4 and 4n12.

[176] Ibid., 20.

The richness of the estate was obvious even a century after Thomas Barclay's death. Following, from a visitor in 1892, is the most detailed eye-witness description we have found:

> A quiet village street ending in an old time shoemakers' shop just over the rail-guarded bridge, across which the street merges into the country highway, glimpses of the Deleware (sic) here and there through the trees, with low-lying meadows between; nothing in sight to suggest the present; such are the surroundings to the home of Mr. John Osborn (sic), a place redolent of colonial times and Revolutionary interests.
>
> At the roadside entrance stands a small lodge house a hip-roofed building quaint in its plainess (sic); part of which the long lane with its triple row of cedars winds up the hill to the well-kept substantial mansion at the top.
>
> The house of two and a half stories facing the river consists of a main building and smaller wing—it is of a yellow color, well toned by time and weather; a broad piazza, a later addition crossed the front; within from the wide hall four large cheerful rooms open, two upon either side; the heavy timbered floors, the paneled doors, the wainscoting (sic) and mouldings particularly, of which the present owner is justly proud so well preserved are they all but substantial witness to the times when solidity was a reality and not an appearance.
>
> From the windows across the sloping fields and shining strip of river lies Trenton with its hazy veil of smoke and present day activity in contrast to its neighbor on the Pennsylvania hillside.
>
> Passing through the hall and out the opposite door the house presents from this side a much quainter appearance; there is an irregularity in the position of the windows, a small hooded porch is over the hall door with its latch and knocker while the wall of the smaller wing is broken by an arched recess opening upon a brick-covered pavement— where at the moment stood several figures, dogs and a horse ready saddled giving a characteristic touch to the place.
>
> To the west an old fashioned high walled garden, the farm buildings and slaves quarters bound the lawn: to Northern eyes the latter are the most interesting and though fast falling to decay enough remains to show what they once were: five tiny cottages open upon a common court of

which the wall of the garden and two other buildings form sides, they are substantially built—of the stone used in other outbuildings upon the place; two rooms are in each house, the lower room has one side entirely taken up with the huge open fire place, oven and soap-boiling arrangements of the times and enclosed staircase leads to the room above which also contains an open fire place—without, the court is paved with flat stones now overgrown with grass and weeds, while a grove of saplings and fruit trees have pushed their way between the stones, making a wilderness where once was heard the songs and mirth of a light-hearted race.

Many interesting ornaments showing the taste of past owners at one time adorned the place; all are long since scattered; a pair of lions now guarding the entrance to St. George's Hall, Philadelphia came from here.[177] But as we saw it one blustry October day, the wind blowing the leaves down in yellow showers it seemed to us the place wanted no other adornment than the beautiful trees which surround it on all sides—tulip poplars, maples, ash, chestnuts dropping their nuts with every wind, tall cedars and pines outlining the lane and mingling their darker foliage with the gay autumn tints on the lawn; they entirely conceal the house, but make a landmark of a place to which each year is adding a new interest.[178]

The twentieth century was not kind to Summerseat (see Appendix D). The estate was a prime property in lower Bucks County until 1919, when it was sold to a developer and subdivided.[179] Three years later, the manor house itself was purchased by the

---

[177] If these are indeed the lions from Summerseat, they can be seen in Robert F. Looney, *Old Philadelphia in Early Photographs 1839-1914: 215 Prints from the Collection of the Free Library of Philadelphia* (New York, 1976), Plate 106, p. 109. Their demise is told in Theodore C. Knauff, *A History of the Society of the Sons of St. George Established at Philadelphia, For the Advice and Assistance of Englishmen in Distress, on Saint George's Day, April 23, 1772...* (Philadelphia, 1923), 57-58. We thank Joseph Benford, Curator, Print and Picture Collection, The Free Library of Philadelphia, and his staff for these two references.

[178] "Visit of Miss Marion Otter of Doylestown to Washington's headquarters Morrisville, Pa. on October 1, 1892," MS dated December 12, 1892, MSL-Summerseat-F1, Spruance Library, BCHS.

[179] Thomas B. Stockham, "Preserving Summerseat, "*Bucks County Papers*, 6 (1932), 53.

Morrisville School District which used it as administrative offices, a gymnasium and home economics classrooms before deciding it was too impractical to maintain. In 1976 it was put up for sale. "No one can accuse the Morrisville school board of being carried away with the Bicentennial Spirit," wrote a local news reporter.[180] Luckily for us, that spirit did move others in Morrisville. The Historic Morrisville Society was formed to buy and save Summerseat and a serious effort was then undertaken to learn more of its history. It was the research of Betty Huber and her late husband, digging into eighteenth century deeds, wills and newspapers that revealed Adam Hoops to be the original owner of Summerseat.

The house itself does hint at its former grandeur. However, without its outbuildings and "the beautiful trees on all sides—tulip poplars, maples, ash, chestnuts...tall cedars and pines outlining the lane..." of which the visitor wrote in 1892, when the estate was already well into its second century, Summerseat today can only hint at the property that was familiar to four prominent eighteenth century owners, as well as to General George Washington, eight Revolutionary War generals, Continental Army soldiers, two Pennsylvania governors, a college president, and Continental Congress delegates.

NOTE

Authors' Note: We owe a deep appreciation to Betty Huber. She unstintingly shared her Summerseat and Morrisville research of twenty years and patiently answered our seemingly endless questions. Her observations and insights have been invaluable. We thank Jane and Jim Murray of the Historic Morrisville Society for showing us around Summerseat and for their generous support in sharing materials from its archives. And we are grateful to John L. Thames and Richard S. Roberts for their substantial inputs to Appendix E.

---

[180] Birgitta Nyholm, "Morrisville's historic Summerseat may go on the block," *Trenton Times*, May 28, 1976. Source courtesy of Betty Huber.

1) Panorama of Summerseat estate taken by William Jackson Pope, Morrisville photographer, circa 1900. Winter scene, showing the extensive outbuildings, with the large stone barn on far left. Summerseat house sits among the pine trees on the right. Historic Morrisville Society Collections.

2) Looking up the lane toward the house. Dated October 1898. On the left is one of the many 18th century outbuildings. Open gate leads to the manor house. Photographer unknown. James E. Wood Collection of Early Morrisville Photographs, Historic Morrisville Society.

3) Stone and wood barn with its striking six columns supporting wood overhang. This unusual barn existed until the early 1900s, when it was demolished to make way for housing lots. This barn appears as background in several early photographs of the Summerseat estate [including the inset with unidentified buildings destroyed in 1970 (photographer unknown)]. Photographer unknown, [William Jackson Pope?] Undated. Historic American Buildings Survey (HABS) No. PA-5345-B, Library of Congress.

4) Remains of Summerseat's slave quarters. "Five tiny cottages open on a common court of which the wall of the garden and two other buildings form sides...two rooms are in each house, the lower room has one side entirely taken up with the huge open fireplace, oven and soap-boiling arrangements...enclosed staircase leads to the room above which also contains an open fireplace." Undated, circa 1890-1910. Photograph by William Jackson Pope (1850-1932). Historic Morrisville Society Collections.

5) One of the outbuildings shown in relation to the Summerseat house. Undated [circa 1890-1905]. Photographer unknown [William Jackson Pope?]. Historic American Buildings Survey (HABS) no. PA-5345-A-3, Library of Congress.

6) Summerseat as it was during the Osborne ownership (1859-1919). The front porch was added sometime during the 19th century. The kitchen wing connected to the house is shown on the right. Arnold Brothers photograph, May 1908. Spruance Library, Bucks County Historical Society.

7) Rear view of Summerseat. Kitchen wing on left, corner of the front porch is visible in lower right corner. Covered entryway was added sometime during 19th century. Arnold Brothers photograph, May 1908. Spruance Library, Bucks County Historical Society.

8) Rear view of Summerseat taken October 1898, showing arch over connecting kitchen wing. Photographer unknown. James E. Wood Collection of Early Morrisville Photographs, Historic Morrisville Society.

9) A somewhat diminished Summerseat from the front, circa 1923. The kitchen wing has been razed and some of the trees have been cut. This is one of the rare photographs showing a lower window in the south wall of the house. Undated, photographer unknown. Historic Morrisville Society Collections.

10) Summerseat in 1924, dwarfed by the new Robert Morris High School built on former Summerseat property. The black strip in the middle of the house shows where the front porch was removed. Most trees have been removed and the white spots seen on the lower north wall of the house are plastered up holes where the kitchen wing had been. Undated [1924]. Photographer unknown. Historic Morrisville Society Collections.

11) Close up of the front of a derelict Summerseat, after removal of front porch and kitchen wing. Circa 1924. Photographer unknown [William Jackson Pope?]. Historic Morrisville Society Collections.

12) A restored Summerseat. October, 1976. Photographer unknown. Historic Morrisville Society Collections.

13) Stairwell and original balustrade inside a restored Summerseat, 1985. Photograph by Jack E. Boucher. Historic American Buildings Survey (HABS) No. PA-5345-12, Library of Congress.

14) First floor back parlor (SW) in a restored Summerseat. Original yellow pine floors. 1985. Photograph by Jack E. Boucher. Historic American Buildings Survey (HABS) No. PA-5345-14, Library of Congress.

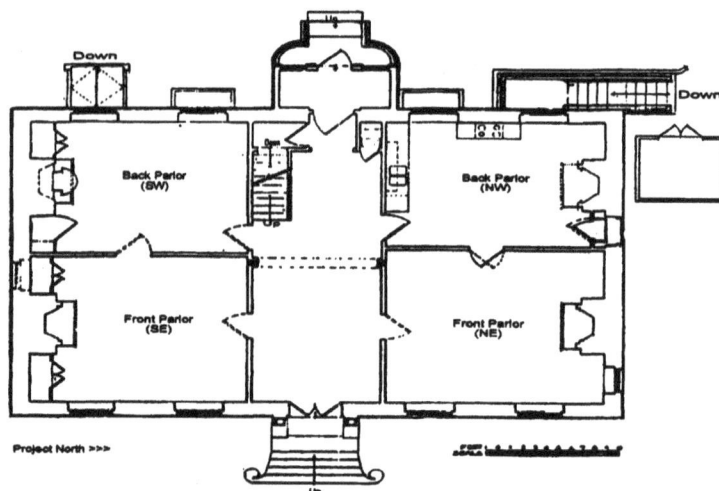

15) Floor plan of Summerseat's first floor. From drawing by architect Peter Andrew Copp. Martin Jay Rosenblum, R.A. & Associates, *Historic Structure Report: Summerseat, 1994*, figure 2.

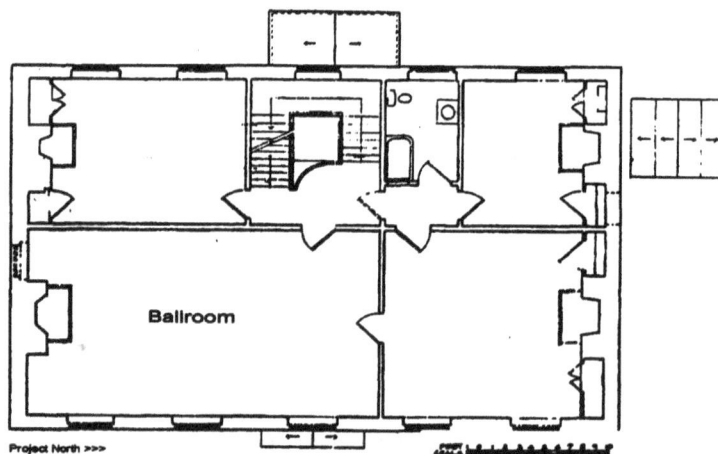

16) Floor plan of Summerseat's second floor. From drawing by architect Peter Andrew Copp. Martin Jay Rosenblum. R.A. & Associates, *Historic Structure Report: Summerseat, 1994*, figure 3.

APPENDIX A
ADAM HOOPS AND BENJAMIN WEST

The painter Benjamin West benefitted from the generosity of several Pennsylvanians during his early years. Chief Justice William Allen is the best known among them. According to Allen's own letters and to Benjamin West himself, he contributed the lion's share of support. The young West was able to travel to Italy, France, and England with funds given by Allen.[1] Other Pennsylvania benefactors are named by Robert C. Alberts, William Dunlap, and James Thomas Flexner.[2] Adam Hoops is not identified by them, but there is a story passed down among descendants of Margaret Hoops Walker (1753/4-1826), youngest daughter of Adam Hoops, that he had "educated Benjamin West, the artist."[3] This is not supported by results of a search through sources on Benjamin West and William Allen, which reveal no mention of Adam Hoops.[4] Moreover, Benjamin West scholars do not cite Hoops as one of his patrons.[5]

---

[1] Norman S. Cohen, "William Allen: Chief Justice of Pennsylvania, 1704-1780," (PhD diss., University of California, Berkeley, 1966), 34-35; E.P. Richardson, "West's Voyage to Italy, 1760, and William Allen," PMHB, 102 (1978):3-26; Robert C. Alberts, *Benjamin West: a Biography* (Boston, 1978), 24-25; 27.

[2] Robert C. Alberts, *Benjamin West: A Biography,* 20-21; William Dunlap, *A History of the Rise and Progress of the Arts of Design in the United States,* 2 vols. (New York, 1834), 1:38,40-41; and James Thomas Flexner, *America's Old Masters,* revised edition, (New York, 1980), 319-322.

[3] Annie Walker Burns, *Family History Records of Dr. Thomas Walker (First Explorer of Kentucky),*(Washington, DC n.d., Reprint with Additions [1964? 1966?]), mimeog. Sections separately paginated, 6:26 and 7:29.

[4] David A. Kimball and Miriam Quinn, eds., "William Allen-Benjamin Chew Correspondence, 1763-1764," *PMHB,* 90(1966):202-226; William Allen Letterbook, 1753-1770, in the HSP; E. P. Richardson, "West's Voyage to Italy, 1760, and William Allen," PMHB, 102 (January 1978), 3-26; Ruth Moser Kistler, "William Allen, Founder of Allentown, Colonial Jurist, Industrialist and Loyalist," *Lehigh County Historical Society Proceedings,* 24 (1962): 47.

[5] John Dillenberger, *Benjamin West, The Context of His Life's Work with Particular Attention to the Paintings with Religious Subject Matter,* (San Antonio, Texas, 1977); William Sawitzky, "The American Work of Benjamin West," *PMHB,* 62 (October 1938):433-462; Helmut von Erffa and Allen Staley, *The Paintings of Benjamin West,* (New Haven, 1986); Dorinda Evans, *Benjamin West and His American Students.* Published for an exhibition at the National Portrait Gallery, October 16, 1980, to January 4, 1981 (Washington, 1980); Allen Staley, "Benjamin West and Pennsylvania," *Benjamin West in Pennsylvania Collections,* published on the occasion

On the other hand, the lives of Hoops, West and the latter's known benefactors did intertwine during the relevant years, and Hoops certainly had both the opportunity and the means to assist the young West. Before dismissing this story as family fable, consider three periods in Benjamin West's life when Adam Hoops could have known and aided him, two in Pennsylvania and one in England.

1. The years 1754-1756.

West is known to have made one or more visits to the town of Lancaster as a teen-ager sometime during the mid-1750s. Eight portraits of prominent Lancaster residents and one historical painting have been identified as West's Lancaster work.[6]

Lancaster was then the westernmost town of any size on the Pennsylvania frontier. Although residing in Carlisle, Adam Hoops was in and out of Lancaster during those years, as a trader, buyer and supplier. Hoops had many business dealings with Edward Shippen, Lancaster's most prominent resident and an associate and relative of William Allen. Shippen, too, was an early benefactor of West. Whether or not Adam Hoops knew of this visiting teen-ager, it is certain that Hoops knew William Henry, the man with whom West boarded in Lancaster. Henry was a gunsmith and was involved in the campaigns of 1755 and 1758 to dislodge the French from the Ohio, as was Adam Hoops. Hoops, like Henry, was a charter member of the Juliana Library Company in Lancaster. Whether Hoops helped out the young West at this time is not known. Although at least two of his daughters are known to have had their portraits painted, we do not know who the artist was or when and where these likenesses were executed.[7]

---

of an exhibition at the Philadelphia Museum of Art, March 1 to April 13, 1986 (Philadelphia, 1986), and essay on Benjamin West in *Benjamin West: American Painter at the English Court*, Catalog of an exhibition held at the Baltimore Museum of Art, June 4-August 20, 1989 (Baltimore, 1989).

[6] William Sawitzky, "The American Work of Benjamin West," *PMHB*, 62 (October 1938), 436-437; James Thomas Flexner, *America's Old Masters*, Appendix, 323; 328-332; Charles I. Landis, "Benjamin West and His Visit to Lancaster," *Lancaster County Historical Society Papers*, 29 (1925):57-61; Allen Staley, essay on Benjamin West, *Benjamin West: American Painter at the English Court*, 14.

[7] Francis Jordan, Jr., *The Life of William Henry of Lancaster, Pennsylvania, 1729-1786, Patriot, Military Officer, Inventor of the Steamboat* (Lancaster, 1910), 39; Charles I. Landis, "The Juliana Library Company in Lancaster," *Historical Papers*

2. The years 1756-1760.

Benjamin West moved to Philadelphia in 1756 from Chester County where he had been born in 1738. He lived three years under the tutelage of the Reverend William Smith, guiding light and first provost of the College and Academy of Philadelphia.[8] Scholars are unsure whether West was an actual student at the College and Academy, but if he was not, he fraternized with boys who were. At the same time that West was being tutored by Reverend Smith, Adam Hoops's oldest son was a student at the College and Academy during these years.[9] William Allen, one of the trustees of the College, also sent his sons there. It would not be at all surprising if William Allen, the most prominent Presbyterian in Pennsylvania, contacted the Hoops and other Presbyterian families to encourage them to enroll their young sons in Reverend Smith's classes in Philadelphia. Or it may have been Reverend Smith himself who contacted Adam Hoops, as it is known that Smith had traveled to Carlisle and Lancaster in the late 1750s. It is possible that Hoops and others were asked to contribute something to West's education during these years. Financially, Hoops was certainly in a position to do so, and Allen, an influential and astute political figure, would have been well aware of this. Although there is no mention of Hoops in William Allen's Letterbook,[10] they were known to each other. Both were members of the First Presbyterian Church on Pine Street.

---

and Addresses of the Lancaster County Historical Society, 33:212-213; Eugenia G. Glazebrook and Preston G. Glazebrook, comps., *Virginia Migrations, Hanover County, 1743-1871*, 2:79, where the "minitures" of Sarah Hoops Syme and Jane Hoops Clark are mentioned in the will of Martha Hoops Syme.

[8] Robert C. Alberts, *Benjamin West*, 19-20; Ann D. Gordon, *The College of Philadelphia, 1749-1779: Impact of an Institution*, (New York, 1989), chapter 4.

[9] Thomas Harrison Montgomery, *A History of the University of Pennsylvania from its Foundation to A.D. 1770* (Philadelphia, 1900), 540.

[10] William Allen Letterbook, 1753-1770, HSP. The authors thank Robert E. Wright, independent researcher at the Historical Society of Pennsylvania for his help with this research. We also appreciate his pointing out the existence of another William Allen Letterbook for the years 1755-1774, consisting primarily of business correspondence. This latter document has not yet been consulted.

3. The year 1763

West went to England after three years study in Italy and France. This is where he would spend the rest of his life, becoming Historical Painter to George III, being elected President of the Royal Academy, and dying there in 1820. However, in 1763, he was an unknown artist, looking for sponsors and commissions. One of his earliest portraits - painted in late 1763 or early 1764 - was that of General Robert Monckton.[11] General Monckton had been commander of forces in America in 1760 and had been in Philadelphia at the time Benjamin West was studying there. During his time in America, Monckton became a close friend of Adam Hoops.[12]

It was in this year, 1763, that General Monckton returned to England, and that both Adam Hoops and his family and William Allen and his daughters visited England. The paths of the Allen and Hoops families crossed at least once there. In October, the Hoops family was at Bath. So was William Allen. Significantly, so was Benjamin West.[13] There is no mention of either Adam Hoops or Benjamin West in the letter William Allen wrote from Bath on October 7, 1763.[14] Adam Hoops, meanwhile, wrote Colonel Bouquet a letter from London on November 6, 1763 that reads in part, "I had the Honour of transmitting the News [of Colonel Bouquet's victory over the Indians] to our worthy friend Mr. Allen, whom I left at Bath about three weeks ago."[15] In this same letter he also gives news of

---

[11] Helmut von Erffa and Allen Staley, *The Paintings of Benjamin West*, 31, 534-535.

[12] Hoops's close ties with Monckton are suggested not only by the letter of 1769 quoted in the text, but also by the fact there was a Monckton portrait at Summerseat. We do not know if this portrait was a copy of West's painting or one of several lithographs made of Monckton in the 18th century. There was also a Monckton Mills noted in the Summerseat inventory. Was this an investment of General Monckton's managed by Hoops or was it a Hoops's property named after his close friend?

[13] Helmut von Erffa and Allen Staley, *The Paintings of Benjamin West*, 24-25; John Galt, *The Life and Works of Benjamin West, Esq. President of the Royal Academy of London, Subsequent to his Arrival in this Country*, 2 vols. (London, 1820), 2:5.

[14] William Allen to Benjamin Chew, Bath Octor. 7th 1763, David A. Kimball & Miriam Quinn, eds., "William Allen-Benjamin Chew Correspondence, 1763-1764," PMHB, 90 (1966): 210-216.

[15] Adam Hoops to Col. Henry Bouquet, 6 November 1763, The Papers of Col. Henry Bouquet, Series 21649, Part. 9, photostat copy in LC.

General Monckton, with whom it is almost certain he visited during his stay in London. How did it come about that General Monckton sat for the young American artist? Von Erffa and Staley quote Wiliam Carey, writing in 1820 that it was through West's brother Samuel, who had fought in the French-Indian War.[16] Staley writes that Monckton "had sought out West because he had known West's brother."[17] May we suggest another possibility? It could have been Adam Hoops, who brought West to Monckton's attention in London in 1763.

The report by Adam Hoops's daughter of his participation in the education of Benjamin West gains plausibility from the fact that Margaret may have been in England with her family in 1763, and may even have met Benjamin West at London and Bath. The trip to Europe was made by "Adam Hoops and family." We do not know which of his eight children accompanied him, but Margaret, who was nine or ten at the time, may have been one of them and may well have passed on this story to her children. Benjamin West himself told his earliest biographer, John Galt, that he had found "on his arrival in London, several American families who had come across the Atlantic after the peace to visit their relations...."[18] The Hoops family was one of these.

The opportunity and the means were there, but Hoops's support of West will remain a family story until documents are discovered to support it.

---

[16] Helmut von Erffa and Allen Staley, *The Paintings of Benjamin West*, 534-535.

[17] Allen Staley, "Benjamin West and Pennsylvania," *Benjamin West in Pennsylvania Collections*, 17.

[18] John Galt, *The Life and Works of Benjamin West*, Pt. 2:3-4.

APPENDIX B

SUMMERSEAT INVENTORY

This is copied from a photocopy of the original fragile manuscript. Punctuation and spelling have been kept as in the original. [...] indicates unintelligible word in original.

Inventory of all & Singular the Goods and Chattles Rights & Credits of Adam Hoops Esq[r] lately deceased at Summerseat in the County of Bucks taken & appraised by Us at Summerseat aforesaid the 2[d] Day of August 1771

Item		£	s	d
1 Dozen Mahogany Chairs red Damask Bottoms			14	8	
1 Mahogany Dining Table			3	
1 ditto Card d°			2	10
1 ditto Tea d°			2	5
1 ditto China d°			4	
1 Japan'd Oval China d°			1	10
1 Pair Brass Fire Irons Shovel & Tongs with Knobs			4	
1 Large Looking Glass			6	
3 Crimson Harrateen Window Curtains	15/		2	5
2 Branches for Candles			1	5
1 Mahogany Bracket				7	6
4 Flower Glasses	2/6			10
1 Hearth Brush				1
1 Mahogany Dining Table			3	
1 C[...] & Bracket			23	
1 Marble Slab			5	
1 Walnut Tea Table				15
10 Bird Pictures	10/		5	
1 Large Looking Glass			6	
1 Pair Fire Irons, Shovel & Tongs with Brass Knobs			4	
1 Hearth Brush				2
1 Dozen High Backed Windsor Chairs			5	
		£	93	18	6

Item		£	s	d
page 2 Amount brought Over		£	93	18	6
1 Mahogany Chest of Drawers			15	
1 Walnut Desk			4	10
1 ditto Chamber Table				15
1 ditto Stand				10
1 Pine Writing Desk				5
1 Broken Looking Glass			3	
1 High posted Bedstead Sacking Bottom and Blue Harrateen Curtains & 3 d° Window d° }			10	
1 Feather Bed Bolster & Pillows Wt 63 lb	2/6		7	17	6
1 Camp Bedsted with Sacking Bottom & Blue Harrateen Curtains }			2	
1 Bed Bolster & Pillows Wt 35 lb	2/		3	10
1 Walnut Closestool Chair			1	10
1 low Stool				1
1 Pair Fire Irons Shovel & Tongs with Brass Knobs			1	6
1 Hearth Brush, 1 Large Windsor Chair 1 Rush Bottom d° }				10
12 Windsor Chairs			5	
1 Marble Slab			5	
1 Large Walnut Dining Table			3	5
1 Walnut Couche, bed & pillow thereunto belonging			2	
1 Lanthern				7
1 Bed Bolster & Pillows Wt 59 lb	20[d]		4	18	4
1 Walnut Chamber Table			1	
1 Pair fire Irons Shovel & Tongs with brass knobs				10
1 Looking Glass gilt Frame			2	10
1 Bedstead and Bottom			1	
d° - - - - - - d°				15
1 Suite Harrateen Curtains & Raised Tester			4	
		£	173	18	4

page 3			£		
Amount brought Over		£	173	18	4
1 Bed Bolster & Pillows wt 70 lb	2/		7		
6 Mahogany Leather Bottom Chairs			6		
1 Wash hand Bason & Stand				15	
1 Toilet Table				5	
1 Looking Glass			4		
1 Mahogany Frame easy Chair coverd wth red Damask			2	10	
6 Roman Antiquities, General Monctons Picture & Cleopatra			3		
1 Pair fire Irons Shovel & Tongs with brass knobs			1		
1 Mahogany Bracket & 3 Flower Glasses				10	
1 English Carpet			3		
2 Walnut Arm Chairs leather Bottoms			2	10	
6 Roman Antiquities			3		
1 Looking Glass gilt Frame			2		
1 Wash hand Bason & Stand				15	
1 Painted Pine Chamber Table			1		
1 Pair fire Irons Shovel & Tongs with brass knobs			1	10	
1 Bedstead, Furniture Check Curtains & 2 Window Curtains of d°			2	10	
1 Bed Bolster & Pillows wt 41 lb	2/6		5	2	6
2 Flower Horns				1	
1 Turkey Carpet			2		
1 Mahogany Chamber Table			4		
1 ditto - - - - - Stand				10	
5 ditto - - - -Chairs			3	15	
1 Rush Bottom Chair				7	6
1 Suite Cotton Curtains			4	10	
1 Bed Stead & Sacking Bottom			1	10	
6 Mahogany Leather Bottom Chairs			5		
		£	240	19	4

page 4			£		
Amount brought Over		£	240	19	4
2 Red Serge Window Curtains				15	
1 Looking Glass			4		
7 Scripture Prints			3	10	
1 Pair fire Irons Shovel & Tongs with Brass knobs & 2 flower horns }				15	
1 Feather Bed wt 55 lb	2/6		6	17	6
2 Marble Slabs			9	12	
1 Cherry Tree Tea Table				15	
12 low back'd Windsor Chairs			6		
2 d° - - - -double d°			2		
1 Bed Bolster & Pillows wt 38 1 d° without pillows - - -------54 } 92 lb	18^d		6	18	
2 Green Harrateen Window Curtains			2		
1 pair double Rose Blankets			2		
3 pair Single - - - -d°			3		
1 Small Bed - - - - - wt 15 lb	18^d		1	2	6
1 Blue & Red Rug			1	10	
4 Old Indian Blankets			1		
1 Pope's head Brush				5	
1 looking Glass			1	15	
4 Old Windsor Chairs				15	
3 large China Bowls			1	16	
2 Soup Dishes				7	6
15 flat - - - - -d°			4		
5 Small Enameld d°				15	
19 Plates			1		
1 TeaPott, 1 Cannister 1 Cream Pott, 1 Slop Bowl 1 Sugar Dish, 9 Cups & Saucers 6 Coffee Cups 1 Spoon 1 Tray Teapott Stand & Butter plate }			1		
		£	304	7	10

page 5

Item		£ s d (mid)	£	s	d
Amount brought Over	£		304	7	10
9 Cups, 11 Saucers, 6 Coffee Cups, 1 Teapott, 1 Cream d°	}		1		
1 Spoon Tray 1 Sugar dish 1 Butter plate 1 Teapott stand					
6 large Enameld Cups & Saucers 2 small d° Bowls	}		1	10	
3 Cups 5 Saucers, 1 Slop Bowl & 4 Saucers					
3 Teapotts, 1 Bowl, 3 dishes 2 Butter Plates	} Queens Ware			10	
1 Teapott and Stand - - - - - - Queens Ware					
16 flat plates 9 d° Soup 4 dishes Delf				16	
16 Wine Glasses 3 Beer d° & 8 Tumblers			1		
12 pewter Water plates	£2 8 0				
5 d° Water dishes	2 10 0				
30 d° plates	1 10 0				
1 d° Soup dish	6				
3 d° Fish dishes & Sieves	15 0		7	9	
3 Cases of Knives & Forks			5		
1 Brass pestle & Mortar				5	
3 Pudding & 13 Petit panns				3	9
1 TeaKettle				15	
1 Coffee Pott				10	
2 Saucepanns				7	6
1 Old Tea Kettle 7/6 - - -1 Old Tea Chest 7/6				15	
1 Spice Box				7	6
1 pair Brass Candlesticks				7	6
1 Pair Steel d°				5	
3 flat Brass d°				3	
7 Iron Potts & Kettles			1	10	
1 Copper Fish Kettle			1	2	6
1 Brass Wash d°				7	6
1 large Iron TeaKettle				12	
	£		329	4	1

page 6

Item			£ s (value)	£	s	d
Amount Brought Over		£		329	4	1
1 Pair Kitchen fire Irons Shovel & Tongs				1		
1 Jack & pullies				2		
1 Toaster, 1 Frying Pan, 2 Cullenders, 14 Tin Cups					5	
3 Earthen Dishes					3	
1 Copper Bakepan				1	10	
1 Funnel, 2 Tin Coffee potts, 1 Chafing Dish					6	
1 flesh fork, 1 ladle, 2 spits, 1 dripping pan						
1 Tin lanthern, 2 Milk Tubs, 4 Wooden Bowls	}			1	5	
2 Siev's 2 1/2 doz. Trenchers 4 pails 2 Buckets a Cooler & 2 Washing Tubs						
2 Small Silver Salvers - - - - - - - - - - - - wt 22 oz		13/		14	6	
4 Candlesticks - - - - - - - - - - - - - - - - 93	13	14/		65	11	1
2 Canns - 17	10	12/		10	10	
4 Salts - 17	6	12/		10	7	7
2 Butter Boats - - - - - - - - - - - £1	10	12/		12	18	
1 Teapott - - - - - - - - - - - - - - - - - - 22		11/		12	2	
1 Pair Snuffers & Stand						
1 Punch Strainer 1 Cream Pott 2 pair Tea Tongs 11 Spoons	} 24	10/		12		
1 Coffee Pott & Soup Spoons - - - - - - - 42	12	15/		31	19	
1 Castor - 41	10	13/		26	19	6
1 Large Tankard - - - - - - - - - - - - - - - - 45	8	12/		27	4	9
1 Small d°- - - - - - - - - - - - - - - - - - - 24	14	10/		12	7	
5 Pair Hames 12/6, 1 Cross CutSaw		20/		1	12	6
2 Saddles				2	10	
1 Cutting Box				1		
1 Post Ax & Dung Fork					8	
1 Roan & 2 Black Horses				30		
		£		607	8	6

APPENDIX B

		£		
page 7	Amount brought Over	607	8	6
14 Load of Hay	46/	28		
a parcle of Oates		1	10	
a parcle of Rye		4		
Trucks & an Old Cart Saddle			8	
Walnut Lumber		2		
2 Grindstones			15	
14 Dress'd Buckskins		8	10	
300 lb - 6^{ny} [sixpenny] Nails		11	5	
Paints & Paint Pott		1		
2 Marble Lyons		7		
6 pair of Sheets	15/	4	10	
6 pair of fine D°		9	8	
3 Cotton Counterpains		2	14	
6 Large Damask Table Cloths		4	10	
12 D° - - - - - - - - - - Napkins		1	4	
12 pair of Pillow Cases		1	16	
1 Silken Bed Quilt		5		
1 Holland d°- - - d°		3		
1 Negroe man named Casar	£ 30			
1 d° - - - - - - - - - - - -Derry	40			
1 d° - - - - - - - - - - - -London	50			
1 Negroe Woman - - - Phillis	36			
1 d° - - - - - - - - - - - -Letitia	0			
1 Negroe Boy 4 years Old - -Jem	10			
1 d°- - - - - - - 2 d°- - - Sambo	10			
1 d°- - - -3 Months- - - Scipio	0			
1 d° Woman - - - - - Dinah	30	206		
1 Cask of Old Iron		1		
	£	910	18	6

		£		
page 8	Amount brought Over	910	18	6
1 Negroe Man Jacko		10		
1 Ditto - - - - -Catoe		70		
1 Ditto - - - - -Jacob		70		
1 Stack of Hay in the New Meadow		4	10	
1 pair of Smiths Bellows		4		
1 Anvil wt 1.3.16 is 212 lb	9^d	7	19	
1 Vice		1	15	
1 Sledge			9	
2 Hammers			3	
4 pair of Smiths Tongs			15	
1 Sett of Shoeing Tools			2	6
1 Screw plate & 4 Taps			10	
3 Steel punches			3	
2 Barrs of Steel & a parcle of Old Iron		1	10	
Barley & the last years Hay, at the Barracks in the Store		8		
1 Batteau		2		
1 Bull		5		
5 Oxen	£ 5	25		
1 Black Cow		4	10	
1 D° - - - - - -with 1 Horn		4		
1 Small Black d°		4		
1 Spotted d°		4		
1 White Calf		1		
20 Sheep & 9 Lambs	7/6	10	17	6
1 Old Waggon		9		
1 New d°		18		
3 Carts		14		
1 Pair of Timber Wheels		7	10	
	£	1199	12	6

page 9			£	1199	12	6
	Amount brought Over					
	5 Old Wheel Barrows				10	
	2 Plows			1	15	
	1 Harrow				15	
	1 Old Slea				5	
	3 Grubbing Hoes				9	
	3 Hassocking Hoes				15	
	5 Axes				15	
	1 Pic-Ax 5 Shovels 3 Crow Barrs 1 Weeding Hoe			1	16	
	6 Pair of Chains	12/		3	12	
	4 Old Spades				12	
	2 Mauls & 5 Wedges				15	
	4 Blind Bridles				12	
	4 Old Pitchforks				5	
	2 Waggon Breeche Bands			2	10	
	1 Cart - - - - - Dº				10	
	7 Horse Collars			1	8	
	2 Old Sledges				5	
	1 Dutch Fann				4	
	1 Chest of Carpenters Tools				4	
	1000 Feet of Plank	5/ per 100		2	10	
	50 Bushels of Slack'd Lime	8ᵈ		1	13	
	10 M. Bricks	22/		11		
	3 Pair of Thill Hames	3/			9	
	1 Gold Watch			20		
	1 Pair of Pistols			5		
			£	1265	13	10

page 10			£	1265	13	10
	Amount brought Over					
	1 Pair of Old Pistls				15	
	1 Large Black Horse & Sulky			35		
	4 Volumes of Burn's Justice of the Peace			2	5	
	Laws of Pennsylvania			2		
	Shallop Summerseat			260		
	1 Old Long Gun			1	10	
	1 Fowling Piece			3		
	1 Negroe Girl named Dinah about 10 Year's Old			35		
				1605	3	10

In Examining the Preceeding Inventory, the following Mistakes were discoved [sic] for & against the Estate

For the Estate						
1 Plate Warmer Omitted	£0 15 0					
1 Rope - - - - - - - - - dº	5					
2 Hopples	8					
1 Perspective Glass & Prints	2 10					
1 Mahogany Tea board	10			4	8	0
				1609	11	10

Against the Estate the following Overcharges						
in the Spice Box in 5th Page	£0.6. 0					
in Milk Panns - - - - - - - - - - - - - - - - - - - :	2. 0		0 8 0		8	0
			£	1609	3	10

s/Thoˢ. Riche

s/Ja. Kirkbride

Note: Some of these furnishings are noted by William MacPherson Hornor, Jr. in his *Blue Book of Philadelphia Furniture: William Penn to George Washington* (Washington, D.C., 1935, Repr. 1977), 38, 130, 155, 230.

APPENDIX C

Transcription of Adam Hoops's properties as listed on the back page of the PENNSYLVANIA GAZETTE, 30 April 1772.

TO BE SOLD,

The following plantations, tracts of land, and houses, &c. being part of the estate of ADAM HOOPS, Esq; deceased:

A tract of land, near Conecocheague creek, in the county of Cumberland, about two miles from Col. Benjamin Chambers's, known by the name of the Locust Land, containing about 600 acres.

A valuable plantation on the great road from Carlisle to Winchester, about two miles above Col. Chambers's, containing about 450 acres of exceeding good wheat and pasture land, including about 60 acres now inclosed for meadow, a great part of which is cleared, and mowed every year; this place was formerly the property of Charles M'Qill, now in the tenure of Mr. Owen Ashton.

A plantation adjoining the above, formerly the property of Patrick Jack, now in the tenure of Andrew Taylor, containing about 460 acres of extraordinary good wheat and meadow land.

Two small tracts of land, one situated on the north side of Conecocheague creek, known by the name of Craig's place; the other on the south side of the said creek, known by the name of Hoops's Mill; these two places are separated by the creek, and contain about 250 acres, of which 30 acres of exceeding good meadow may be made: On each of the two last mentioned places is a very fine mill seat.

A plantation on the great road leading from Carlisle to Winchester, adjoining the plantation formerly belonging to John Mushels, containing about 600 acres of good land, of which about 20 acres of excellent good meadow (sowed with timothy seed) is already made, and 30 acres more may be made; this is well situated for a store or tavern.

A tract or plantation on Conecocheague creek, formerly called Spear's place, about two miles below the house of John Alleson, Esq; and adjoining the plantation of Mr. Henry Pawling, containing about 300 acres.

A plantation of about 300 acres, adjoining the last described tract.

The above plantations and tracts of land are situated in a very thriving, thick settled, and well improved county, about 80 miles from Baltimore-Town, in Maryland, and much nearer to the navigable parts of Patowmack.

A very valuable plantation, situate on Letort's Spring, about half a mile from the town of Carlisle, containing about 230 acres of fine wheat land, of which about 45 acres are clear; this place may be disposed of to great advantage by laying it out into lots for the inhabitants of Carlisle.

A large well finished stone house, two stories high, 4 rooms on a floor, with a good stone kitchen, stable, &c. now in the tenure of Mr. George Stevenson.

A tract of land within 4 miles of Bedford, containing between 300 and 400 acres, known by the name of the Long Bottom, adjoining the Turkey Bottom; this tract is fit for raising hemp, or for meadows, and having a fine stream of water running through it, water-works may be very conveniently erected there.

A plantation and tract of land, called Summerseat, pleasantly situated on the river Delaware, near the falls of Trenton, in the county of Bucks, containing 220 acres, or thereabouts, of which 125 acres are clear, including 40 acres of good meadow, the rest woodland; there is a large new and well finished brick house, kitchen, stone barn, stables, and other offices erected on the premises----also two young orchards, and two dwelling houses, at one of which is kept a store, the whole in good repair. At this place is caught, in the season, great quantities of shad, herring, sturgeon, rock, and perch; its situation renders it one of the most agreeable seats on Delaware, being at the head of tide-water, only 29 miles from Philadelphia, and not 100 yards from the post road between the latter and New-York. A town at this place is much wished for, and the purchaser may lay out a few acres in lots, to the greatest advantage in that part which lies most contiguous to the ferry.

An Island, containing 40 acres of excellent land; and 20 acres opposite thereto, and adjoining the above described plantation, whereon is erected a compleat merchant mill, 60 x 54 feet, accommodated with one pair of burr, one pair of Cologne, and one pair of country stones, with scales and weights, a rolling screen, boulting works and hoisting geers, all going by water. A handsome two story frame dwelling house, a kitchen, stone stable, and barn;---two stone tenements, which may lett for Fifteen Pounds per annum;---a smith's shop, with bellows, anvil, and other necessary tools. A sloop, that carried 320 barrels of flour, may load within 200 yards of the mill tail. This mill has the advantage of being almost fully supplied with wheat from Durham and the Minisinks, as the boats may, without passing through the falls, come into the dam, and deliver their grain almost at the mill door.

A small plantation, containing about 66 acres, part of which is meadow, situated at the Upper Cross-roads, in Baltimore county, Maryland, now in the tenure of Mr. G. Stuart; on this place are built a good house, stables, shed, &c. it is noted for the best stand in Baltimore county for a store and tavern.

A dwelling-house, range of stores, and wharff, on the north side of Market-street, Philadelphia, adjoining to and extending from the house of Mr. Joseph Donaldson to the river Delaware, containing in front about 90 feet; the stores consist of three on the ground floor, two on the floor above, and a sail-loft over the whole. For terms of sale, apply to MRS. ELIZABETH HOOPS, to ROBERT and DAVID HOOPS, at Summerseat, near Trenton Ferry, to DANIEL CLARK, at Clover Hill, or to THOMAS BARCLAY, in Philadelphia, who request the favour of all persons who are indebted to the estate of the said A D A M H O O P S, to make immediate payment to either of them; and those who have demands against said estate, are desired to bring in their accounts, that they may be adjusted and paid.

 DANL CLARK
 THOS BARCLAY
  Trustees

 ELIZABETH HOOPS, Executrix
 ROBERT HOOPS, Executor
 DAVID HOOPS, Executor

APPENDIX D

SUMMERSEAT IN THE TWENTIETH CENTURY

Summerseat's history had slipped away from the memory of most Pennsylvanians in the late nineteenth century, when William W. H. Davis sought to resurrect it. In October 1892, while researching the second edition of his massive history of Bucks County, Davis sent Miss Marion Otter of Doylestown to visit the Osborne place, where rumor had it Washington had spent some time.[1]

Her elegiac report, describing an other-worldly pre-industrial pastoral scene, was cited in its entirety at the end of our article. Davis may also have been responsible for persuading owner John H. Osborne to write down a few lines about the historic house in 1879. Entitling it "Washington at Trenton Falls in 1776," Osborne recalled

> at the time he bought the property, [the house]] had been standing 108 years, is 45 x 60 feet, walls part stone and part brick...the woodwork through the house is of yellow pine of the best quality. The large hall doors and other doors through the house swing on the original strap hinges that look as if they had been pounded into shape on an anvil by a country blacksmith....[2]

Around the turn of the century, Doylestown philanthropist, Henry Chapman Mercer, began taking an interest in Bucks County's old buildings. An obsessive collector, archaeologist, developer of the Moravian Pottery and Tile Works, builder of the idiosyncratic

---

[1] William W. H. Davis, *History of Bucks County Pennsylvania from the discovery of the Delaware to the Present Time* (New York, 1905), 3 vols. 2nd ed. revised and enlarged...under supervision of Warren S. Ely and John W. Jordan, 2:168-169.

[2] "Washington at Trenton Falls in 1776," two-page manuscript written by John H. Osborne, undated [1879], Spruance Library, BCHS, MSL-Summerseat-F1. Osborne continues, "The house now, after 128 years, is sound and good and looks as if it would stand the wear of 200 years longer. The open stove in one of the chambers was cast by Isaac Potts in 1795...." This fireplace can still be seen at Summerseat. It is reproduced in National Society of the Colonial Dames of America (Pennsylvania*), Forges and Furnances in the Province of Philadelphia,* (Philadelphia, 1914), unpaginated.

concrete castle named Fonthill, and a founder of the Bucks County Historical Society, Mercer spent the next several decades searching for and documenting the tools, implements and simple objects used by early Pennsylvanians in building their dwelling houses.[3] Summerseat was among the "about one hundred and twenty old houses" he visited for his book, *The Dating of Old Houses*.[4] Mercer had photographs taken in 1903 of the "downstairs halls and several interior rooms," sent his associates in 1919 to do a survey of the house, had plaster casts of moldings made, and wrote the Historical Society of Pennsylvania, urging it "to save from destruction the old house of Robert Morris opposite Trenton, known as Summerseat."[5]

---

[3] Henry Chapman Mercer (1856-1930) has received much scholarly attention. The most comprehensive biography is Cleota Reed, *Henry Chapman Mercer and the Moravian Pottery and Tile Works*, (Philadelphia, 1996 paperback edition), but see also B. F. Fackenthal, Jr., "Dr. Henry Chapman Mercer, Biographical," *The Bible in Iron or Pictured Stoves and Stove Plates of the Pennsylvania Germans* by Henry C. Mercer (Doylestown, Pa., 1941), 2nd ed. by Horace M. Mann, unpaginated. For his early interest in historic preservation see Steven Conn, "Henry Chapman Mercer and the Search for American History," PMHB, 116, no.3 (July 1992), 323-355; Aaron Siskind, *Bucks County Photographs of Early Architecture* with text by William Morgan (Bucks County Historical Society, 1974), 12-14; Cory M. Amsler, "Henry Mercer and the Dating of Old Houses," *Mercer Mosaic* 6 (no. 1, winter 1989), 18-28; and Karen Lucic, *Charles Sheeler in Doylestown: American Modernism and the Pennsylvania Tradition* (Allentown, Pa., 1997), 18-19.

[4] So it says on page one. On page 28, Mercer states he examined "at least one hundred and fifty houses." *The Dating of Old Houses: A Paper Read by Dr. Henry C. Mercer, of Doylestown, Pa. at a Meeting of The Bucks County Historical Society at New Hope, Bucks County, Pa., October 13, 1923* (From BCHS Papers, Vol. 5), Doylestown, 1923. Summerseat is not mentioned by name in this edition. The Historic Structure Report (hereafter HSR) cites a "1919 Survey by the Henry C. Mercer Associates." These associates, Benjamin H. Barnes, Mercer's chauffeur, and Frank King Swain, his manager and general factotum, came to Summerseat on 30 November 1919 and surveyed the manor house and the kitchen wing. The transcribed field notes, cited in the HSR as *The Dating of Old Houses* (1946 BCHS edition), pp. 298-304, are bound typewritten notes and have not been published. Martin Jay Rosenblum R.A. & Associates, *Historic Structure Report: Summerseat*, 29-30.

[5] Letter from Henry C. Mercer to Hampton Carson of the Historical Society of Pennsylvania, February 13, 1926, cited in the Historic Morrisville Society Newsletter of July 1994 printed in *Historical Tales: Tantalizing Tidbits of History from Historic Morrisville Society Newsletters*, eds. James A. Murray and Gretchen Leahy,[Morrisville, Pa., n.d.], 23-24. The 1903 photographs are listed in "List of Prints Mounted in Albums up to August 1, 1917," *A Collection of Papers Read Before the Bucks County Historical Society*, vol. 4 (1917), 756-757. This latter

(continued...)

With the death of John H. Osborne in August 1894 began ten years of legal transactions, which resulted in the final breakup of the estate. These legal complexities involved the selling of Summerseat at public vendue in 1895 to liquidate John H. Osborne's debts, one of the heirs buying it back, the title changing hands within the family and a power of attorney granted to daughter Ada Isabella Osborne in 1897.[6] Of the two surviving Osborne children who grew up at Summerseat, Charles Churchill Osborne had moved to London in the 1880s, leaving his sister Ada Isabella (Mrs. Richard Humphrey Graves Osborne) as châtelaine at Summerseat (their mother had died in 1881).[7] It was Ada who had the estate surveyed and plotted into small lots. The sale of these lots began in 1901 and continued with parcels being sold annually until 1919, when the remaining 126 acres of the Summerseat estate were sold to a Trenton developer. [8] Eight

---

(...continued)
source courtesy of Betty Huber.

[6] Bucks County Deed Book 276, "William Simpson, Clerk of Orphans' Court to Chas. Churchill Osborne," pp. 319-324, 26 January 1897; Bucks County Deed Book 280, "Executors of John H. Osborne and Ada Isabella Osborne to Charles Churchill Osborne," pp. 52-56, 5 February 1897; Bucks County Deed Book 296, "Letter of Attorney Charles C. Osborne and wife to Ada Isabella Osborne," pp. 460-463, 5 October 1897; Bucks County Deed Book 318, "Charles C. Osborne to Ada Isabella Osborne," pp. 428-432, 12 August 1904. We thank Betty Huber for sharing her research into all these deeds.

[7] John H. Osborne, born in 1820 in County Kilkenny, Ireland of an Anglo-Irish family, had emigrated to the United States in 1840, had gone to work in New York state for a railroad company, and in 1845 was appointed chief engineer of the Philadelphia and Reading Railroad Company. In Philadelphia he met and married the young widow Lydia Collins Pawling (1816-1881). Both of his children married Osbornes. Charles Churchill Osborne (1859 - ?) married Lucy Caulfield Osborne (d. 1910) and Ada Isabella Osborne married Dr. Richard Humphrey Graves Osborne (1848-1929). Richard and Lucy were brother and sister, children of Richard Boyse Osborne (1815-1899), their father's older brother, making them all first cousins. J. A. C. Osborne, Notes [on Diary of R. B. Osborne], typescript and manuscript in National Library of Ireland, Dublin, microfilm copy available through interlibrary loan from the National Museum of American History library, mfm 991, NMAH; Charles Churchill Osborne, Philip Bourke Marston (London, 1926), 28; Richard Humphrey Osborne obituary, New York Times, June 10, 1929; biographical information on Richard Humphrey Graves Osborne from the University of Pennsylvania archives, e-mail from Martin J. Hackett, public affairs archivist, April 30, 1999.

[8] Bucks County Deed Book 426, "Agreement of Sale Ada I. Osborne to Isaiah Birks," pp. 432-433, 23 October 1919; Bucks County Deed Book 421, "Ada Isabella

(continued...)

months later the Washington Heights Realty Company of Morrisville gained title to the land, including the manor house, and immediately started clearing the two hundred year old trees , dismantling the stone outbuildings and laying out streets.[9] Saving the old Osborne House, as it was then known locally, was not in the plans of the realty company, but it allowed it to stand temporarily, renting it to the Willet C. Sanford Post of the American Legion.[10]

(...continued)
Osborne to Isaiah Birks," pp. 460-464, 15 December 1919. Twenty-five parcels of land are listed in this deed, with the names of the buyers and the dates purchased. Deeds courtesy of Betty Huber.

[9] Bucks County Deed Book 435, "Isaiah Birks to Washington Heights Realty Company," pp. 495-499, 4 September 1920. Source courtesy of Betty Huber.

[10] There is a curious lack of documentation concerning the American Legion occupation of Summerseat. The School Board minutes and Thomas B. Stockham, Jr. in his article (p. 55) lead one to believe that the American Legion owned the building - "That Building Committee interview Mr. Baker & ascertain his price for the site of land known as the American Legion Plot" (School Board minutes January 12, 1922) and "That Secretary notify Mr. Charles Henry Baker that his proposition of $15,000 for the American Legion site be refused as the price was deemed exorbitant" (School Board minutes February 6,1922). Harry J. Podmore, columnist and photographer for the *State Gazette* newspaper (Trenton, NJ), wrote also about the American Legion purchase in his article, "'Summerseat,' Morrisville's Shrine Will be Preserved," *State Gazette*, September 24, 1920. ("The mansion, which is the finest specimen of Colonial residence in Bucks county, has at last been spared as an historic shrine for the coming generations by its purchase recently by the Willet C. Sanford Post of the American Legion, which is now having the interior renovated for a future home. This purchase was a timely one, as the effects of the work of the vandal and tooth of time were already making their presence known."). However, indefatigable researcher Betty Huber has found no deed of sale in the name of the American Legion, nor any mention of Summerseat in local American Legion records. On June 14, 1922 the School Board minutes record "That we purchase from the Washington Heights Realty Co the tract of land known as the American Legion site...containing about 4 acres of land for the price of $8000...." In June and August 1922 minutes the building is referred to as Legion Hall, but in September the minutes note "new desks [were] installed in Osborn School." Whoever the owner, the American Legion did use it as a clubhouse, and goodness knows what else, sometime between mid-1920 and mid-1922. (On June 28, 1921, the Morrisville High School Senior Class held its commencement exercises there, "Admit Bearer to Commencement Exercises of the Class of 1921 Morrisville High School Tues. June 28, 8 p.m. American Legion Hall, Morrisville, Pa," files of HMS). When the Washington Heights Realty Company began developing its Summerseat lands, they hired a man by the name of Steiner as project manager. The Steiner family, which included two children, lived in Summerseat, while their father "put in all the streets using horse & wagons. Cut down & dynamited all the big trees and sawed them by hand." Both of these
(continued...)

In 1922, the Morrisville School District purchased from the Washington Heights Realty Company four acres of Summerseat property, including the Osborne house[11] The District immediately set about putting the Osborne house in shape for classrooms and began clearing the land in preparation for construction of the Robert Morris High School.[12]

The house by this time had undergone several changes to its original eighteenth-century design. The original stone kitchen building, which may have been the oldest structure on the property, perhaps dating back to the early 1700s, had been connected to the main house sometime during either the Clymer (1798-1812) or Waddell residency (1812-1859). Photographs taken in the 1890s show the archway connecting the two structures. This kitchen wing, with a second story and attic or garret added some time, supposedly during the nineteenth century, was demolished in 1924 by the School District.. ("Mr. Bray...is to grade the grounds and fill the top of the foundation excavation with loam").[13] A long porch supported by six columns was added along the front facade and the first floor windows were extended to the floor.

Repairs were periodically made, but it became increasingly clear to the School Board that maintaining the Osborne school, as it was now called, was becoming costly. The razing of the kitchen wing having left a gaping hole in the north wall, the Board was afraid "that tramps will get in through this hole, set fire to the old building and so burn down their school house." Realizing the old building could

---

(...continued)
children seventy years later shared their memories of living in the old mansion, commenting that when they moved out, "the American Legion took over." Letter from Charles "Red" Steiner to Mr. and Mrs. Robert Habel, 5 March 1990, HMS files, quoted in *Historical Tales:Tantalizing Tidbits of History*, 24; "Report on a Visit to Summerseat June 23, 1980 made by Sarah Steiner Curtin, aged 72," five-page handwritten notes recorded by Betty Huber, HMS files; Rosenblum R.A. & Associates, *Historic Structure Report: Summerseat*, 31.

[11] Bucks County Deed Book 471, pp. 183-185, 22 July 1922.

[12] This high school, built in 1924, burned in 1958. James A. Murray, Jr., *Morrisville* (Dover, NH, 1997), Images of America series, 50.

[13] School Board minutes, March 12, 1924, p. 122. The School Board information cited in these footnotes is taken from an 8-page typewritten synopsis of the minutes copied by Betty Huber from the original handwritten ledgers on deposit at the HMS. See also Rosenblum R.A. & Associates, *Historic Structure Report: Summerseat*, 15, 16-17.

never be turned into a functional modern school within the constraints of their budget, they decided "to pull it down this spring and erect a small monument to Robert Morris in its place." [14]

Enter Thomas B. Stockham, Jr., who became Morrisville's most prominent citizen by the time of his death in 1948. Stockham in 1925 headed a committee from the Morrisville Chamber of Commerce to stay the forces of destruction. At a School Board meeting in March 1925 this committee, along with the Washington Crossing Park Commission, implored the members to save the old Osborne building. Their plea was heeded and the Morrisville Chamber of Commerce was granted an extension until November 1, 1925 to come up with funds to begin restoration. [15]

The historic building by this time badly needed restoring. The north wall had that hole in it where the kitchen wing had been razed. The roof needed shoring up, inside and outside walls needed masonry work, plaster ceilings were cracked and falling, peeling wallpaper needed to be stripped, chimneys needed rebuilding, doors and windows needed new frames and panels, spindles on the balustrade were broken or missing, and there was no central heating. [16]

From 1925 until his death in 1948, Thomas B. Stockham Jr. worked diligently to restore the Osborne building. As Mayor of Morrisville, as President of the Chamber of Commerce, as President of the School Board, as an elected assemblyman to the Pennsylvania House of Representatives from Bucks County, he talked to every one he knew - and he knew everyone - and used every leverage to obtain funds and support for this historic structure. From the article he wrote in 1926 imploring Pennsylvanians to preserve Summerseat to

[14] Letter from Henry C. Mercer to Hampton Carson, February 13,1926, cited in *Historical Tales: Tantalizing Tidbits of History from Historic Morrisville Society Newsletters*, 23-24.

[15] School Board minutes, May 13 and May 24, 1925, pp. 151-152, HMS files. Thomas B. Stockham's career can be followed in George P. Donehoo, ed., *Pennsylvania, a History* (New York, 1926), 115; *Pennsylvania Manual, 1935-1936* (Harrisburg, 1936), 318-319, and *Pennsylvania Manual, 1947-1948,* "Biographical Sketches of Representatives," (Harrisburg, 1948); *Morrisville Herald,* January 13, 1938; April 20, 1945; April 26, 1946; June 11, 1948; and *New York Times,* January 15, 1936; June 6, 1948.

[16] "General Specifications for the Renovation [of the] Osborne Mansion," issued by Board of Education of the Borough of Morrisville, Bucks County, Pennsylvania, and Thomas B. Stockham, Morrisville, Pa., n.d. [1930], HMS files.

obtaining a grant from the Pennsylvania Department of Public Instruction in 1930 to finance restoration, Stockham kept the issue of Summerseat's historic preservation alive.[17] It may have been at Stockham's suggestion that the School Board officially voted in 1931 that the Osborne building "be named Summerseat in the future." He also was consulted by the Pennsylvania Historical Commission on the wording of the historical marker, which was erected at the house on January 29, 1949.[18]

By 1976 the School Board had decided to sell Summerseat ("It's really the best year to sell it"). Strapped for money, the School Board found "Summerseat is costly to insure, heat and maintain." Although "it's just a shell of a building where someone once stayed," occasional tourists would show up at the door, because of that someone who once stayed there. "In fact we had 25 to 30 people here on Washington's birthday from New Jersey, Maryland and Virginia. They were kind of embarrassed when they found out it was offices and not what they wanted it to be. It's a shame we don't have the money to keep it as an historic site," commented the School

---

[17] Thomas B. Stockham, "Preserving 'Summerseat'", *Bucks County Papers*, 6 (1932), 53-57. Efforts to learn more about this grant were unavailing. Louis M. Waddell, archivist at the Pennsylvania State Archives, searched Record Group 22, Records of the Department of Education, Office of the Comptroller, Division of School Accounting. Of the seventy-one cartons of school district annual reports for the years, 1920-1972, every fifth year had been preserved. Although 1930-31 was one of the five-year reporting dates, the Bucks County report was missing. He also searched the records of the School Plant Division of the Bureau of School Administration in the Department of Public Instruction (former name of Department of Education). There was nothing on the Osborne House, Summerseat, or even on Morrisville. According to Thomas B. Stockham, Jr.'s grandson, the Pennsylvania Department of Labor and Industry approved the "renovation drawings" for Summerseat. (Communication from Ronald L. Stockham to the authors, April 13, 1999). In Record Group 16 the Department Bulletin Books, Minute Books of the Industrial Board, Monthly Bulletin Books, Report Files, and Special 'Bulletin' Books of that Department were also searched for reference to appropriations for rebuilding old school buildings. Again, nothing was found pertaining to Summerseat. We are very grateful to Dr. Waddell for his efforts on our behalf.

[18] Correspondence between S. K. Stevens, State Historian, and Thomas B. Stockham, August 30-September 4, 1946. Originals in Record Group 13: Records of the Historical and Museum Commission, Bureau of Archives and History. Historical Marker Files, 1914-1955 (Carton 12, folder 14) in the Pennsylvania State Archives, Division of Archives and Manuscripts, Pennsylvania Historical and Museum Commission. We thank George R. Beyer for these references.

Superintendent.[19]   But the School Board was not a historical society and Summerseat went on the market.

The intended sale of the historic house was the catalyst for the formation of the Historic Morrisville Society.   Incorporated on September 21, 1976 "to promote understanding and appreciation of the history of Morrisville with greatest emphasis on the Colonial and Revolutionary periods,"[20]   the Historic Morrisville Society purchased the building in 1980 and remains its owner today.   Summerseat's preservation has been assured, but much about it remains obscure.

Unlike other eighteenth-century country seats and Georgian houses in the greater Philadelphia area that have been the subject of detailed studies by historians and scholars, Summerseat has no recorded design history. The earliest illustrations—black and white photographs—date from 1886, when it was well over one hundred years old. The two known sketch maps are also recent. These maps dated 1891 and c. 1920 show the location of some of the outbuildings in relation to the manor house and are of historical interest.[21] Detailed architectural and structural analyses by Peter Andrew Copp

---

[19] Birgitta Nyholm, "Morrisville's historic Summerseat may go on the block," *Trenton Times*, May 28,1976.

[20] *Bucks County Law Reporter*, October 14, 1976. Source courtesy of Betty Huber.

[21] Early photographs of Summerseat can be found at several locations. The Historic Morrisville Society owns two collections of early Morrisville photographs: the Mabel Whittaker Collection of William Jackson Pope negatives and photographs and the James E. Wood Collection of late nineteenth and early twentieth century photographs of Morrisville. Most of the early photographs of Summerseat were taken by Mabel Whittaker's grandfather, William Jackson Pope. Pope, who emigrated to Morrisville from Hanley, Staffordshire, England in 1869, became the unofficial photographer of the borough during his residence of sixty-three years. A long-time employee of the Robertson Art Tile Company, Pope was also the borough lamplighter during the days when the streets were lighted by gas lamps and was at one time Burgess of Morrisville. He died on September 10, 1932 at the age of eighty-two, leaving hundreds of glass plate negatives. Other photographs of Summerseat are those taken by Jack E. Boucher for the Historic American Buildings Survey (HABS No. PA-5345) in the Library of Congress Print Department.   Copies of these HABS prints are also in the Pennsylvania State Archives. Other prints can be found at the Spruance Library (BCHS), the Free Library of Philadelphia, and in private Morrisville collections. The two sketch maps are in the HMS files: the 1891 map is part of the will and inventory of John H. Osborne, Will no. 19283, Bucks County Register of Wills, and the c1920 map was an enclosure in a letter from Charles "Red" Steiner to Mr. and Mrs. Robert Habel, 5 March 1990, cited in *Historical Tales:Tantalizing Tidbits of History*, p. 24. See also "List of Prints Mounted in Albums up to August 1, 1917," *A Collection of Papers Read Before the Bucks County Historical Society*, vol. 4 (1917), 756-57, for eight views of "The Osborne House, in 1903, Morrisville, Pa."

for Martin Jay Rosenblum R.A. & Associates in 1994 can be found in the Historic Structure Report. Although important new information was uncovered during structural reinforcement undertaken in 1995 regarding room sizes and original (pre-1930) finishes,[22] further research is needed to date the various changes to the building. The report shows conclusively that the interior of the building has much of historical interest.

Outside there is much of historical interest also. That artifacts are buried in the grounds of Summerseat is clear from the results of an archeological excavation of 1986. Barbara Liggett retrieved hand-wrought headed nails (was the spirit of Henry Mercer guiding her hand?) and brown glazed and plain glazed earthenware, which she dated c. 1740-1760. Some handblown bottles were located at the north rear corner of the house, where she estimated more artifacts would be found. "The house proper has a high potential...for retreival (sic) of historic archeological materials," she wrote in her report, and although the kitchen wing had long been demolished, the "kitchen addition foundations were located during the preliminary excavations, and can be fully exposed." Significant materials were retrieved from the front of Summerseat near the stone steps, such as "salt-glazed stoneware" and green bottle fragments which she dated c. 1740-1765. Alongside the driveway in back she found "many artifacts, all very small and exclusively creamwares, from 1765 hand painted cream-colored earthenware to Leeds 1780 commercial production, some wine glass fragments, all good quality." Dr. Liggett's report suggests other promising sites at Summerseat for archeological investigation.[23]

The Historic Structure Report concludes that Summerseat "deserves the best in care, preserving what does remain, so that the house can be used as the background for interpretation the lives (sic) of all the people who lived at Summerseat."[24] To aid in this interpretation, several yet to be consulted documentary collections may yield information on Summerseat's long history. George Clymer's letters with his son Henry Clymer (who lived in Summerseat from 1798 to 1812) and the voluminous Pemberton papers in the Historical Society of Pennsylvania might profitably be consulted for mention of Summerseat. The fifth owner of Summerseat was Elizabeth

---

[22] Communication to the authors from Peter Andrew Copp, May 18, 1999.

[23] Barbara Liggett, *Report on Investigations at Summerseat*, Morrisville, 6-9.

[24] Rosenblum R.A. & Associates, *Historic Structure Report: Summerseat*, 20.

Pemberton Waddell, daughter of Joseph Pemberton (1745-1782) and granddaughter of Israel Pemberton, Jr. (1715-1779). The private correspondence of Robert Morris for the years 1791-1798 may provide clues to which Morris family member, if any, actually resided at Summerseat during the 1790s.[25] A search through the Henry Mercer papers and the Fonthill Manuscripts at the Bucks County Historical Society may provide additional material on the manor house, while the scattered correspondence of Thomas Fitzsimmons, (1741-1811) who jointly with George Clymer financed the purchase of the estate from the bankrupt Robert Morris, may reveal some useful formation. In the voluminous Papers of James Wilson (1742-1798) there is a "Draught of Part of Thomas Barckleys Land," a survey of thirty of Summerseat's acres.[26] If Wilson was considering speculating on the Summerseat property, there may be pertinent documents in this manuscript collection.

Contemporaneous with Adam Hoops's Summerseat (which he spelled variously Summerset or Somerset) was another country seat called Somerset. Lynford Lardner (1715-1774) and his wife Elizabeth Branson Lardner built that Somerset on the Delaware River north of Philadelphia in the 1750s. Adam Hoops's townhouse was one block from Lardner's and it bordered on property owned by Mrs. Lardner's father. They obviously knew each other. Research in the several Lardner collections might allow one to determine whether Hoops was inspired by the Lardner country seat.[27]

---

[25] The Papers of Robert Morris: Private Letter Book, vol. 1: December 22, 1794 through May 19, 1796 (microfilm edition, reel 9) was consulted at the Library of Congress. Other collections of private Morris letters (not consulted) are located at the Historical Society of Pennsylvania, American Philosophical Society Library (in the Sol Feinstone Collection of The David Library of the American Revolution), Henry E. Huntington Library and the New York Public Library.

[26]Papers of James Wilson, vol. 8, pp. 6-7, HSP.

[27]Jack L. Lindsey, "Lynford Lardner's Silver: Early Rococo in Philadelphia," *Magazine Antiques*, April 1993, 608-615, with illustration of Somerset on p. 612; Lynford Lardner Account Book and Day Book, 1748-1751, Rosenbach Museum and Library, Philadelphia; Lardner Papers, HSP; and Will no. 52, 1774 in Office of Recorder of Wills, Philadelphia City Hall.

APPENDIX E

MAPPING SUMMERSEAT

The Summerseat estate property was built up over a three year period in which Adam Hoops purchased three plots of land: 70 acres (plus a 30 acre island) in 1764,   3 acres in 1765, 174 acres in 1766.

To obtain an appreciation of the original Summerseat holdings relative to the present property and its surroundings, we created a map of the original property and overlaid it on 19th and 20th century maps of Morrisville.   The results make it clear that the house known as Summerseat was on the plot purchased in 1766 and show that the land Hoops purchased in those three years covered a significant part of what is now Morrisville.

The purpose of the present appendix is to identify the sources of information used to prepare and overlay these figures, and the issues confronted and their resolution.

Sources

The principal sources of information were deeds and maps. Basic data defining the property came from the deeds concerning the purchases in 1764, 1765 and 1766.[1] Deeds related to the subsequent sale of this land to Thomas Barclay and to later dispositions of parts of it were used to find references that could help position the property on the map. They also proved useful to verify the measurements in the earlier deeds. Each deed conveying a piece of property defines the borders in terms of distances and directions from the starting point, then from each corner to the next. This is basic data needed to outline a property. In many cases the deeds also mention landmarks, prior owners, neighboring owners and other such characteristics that help locate the property in relation to its surroundings.

The maps themselves also provide useful information when it comes to placing the property outline on them. We used two maps: an 1876 map of Morrisville Borough which shows the Summerseat

---

[1] Josiah Wood to Adam Hoops, August 14, 1764, Bucks County Deed Book 15, pp.12-15;   William Morris & Wife to Adam Hoops, August 3, 1765, Bucks County Deed Book 11, pp.661-662; Benjamin Wood & Wife to Adam Hoops, December 2, 1766, Bucks County Deed Book 15, pp.15-18.

house and outbuildings, and relevant landmarks.[2]
- a 1981 US Geological Survey (USGS) map showing contemporary Morrisville and the surrounding region.[3]

Issues

There arose three issues related to mapping Hoops's purchases of 1764-1766 and placing them on maps of the area.

1. The survey data defining the plots when Hoops bought them do not always agree with the definitions on later deeds where the latter clearly appear to be describing the same pieces of property. This is particularly the case with the 1773 deed for Thomas Barclay's purchase of much of the property from the Hoops estate and a later transfer from Barclay's creditors to Robert Morris.[4] The differences are evident in the table in Figure 1.

    Each border segment and the deed in which it is defined is identified by a letter appearing in the "code" column; a letter in the "match" column (found only for the 1773 deed) identifies a corresponding border segment defined in one of the earlier deeds. For example, consider the border segments coded "L" and "M", and those coded "j" and "k". Segments L and M (of the 174 acre 1766 deed) correspond with segments "j" and "k" (of the 1773 deed for Barclay's purchase of the land from the Hoops estate). In this example, "L" and "j" begin at roughly the same place, ("roughly" because they follow segments "K" and "i" which differ in length, 3,696 vs 3,762 feet), and "k" and "M" both end at the same place, "a stone set were (sic) formerly stood a black oak marked for a corner."[5] However, "j" is 35 perches (577 feet) longer than "L" and the orientations of "k" (N18°W) and "M" (N15°W) are slightly different.

[2] J.D. Scott. *Combination Atlas Map of Bucks County, Pennsylvania* "Borough Map of Morrisville" [1876] [G1263. B8S4 1876 fol. Plates 40 & 41]. Original in collection of the Geography and Map Division, Library of Congress.

[3] U.S. Geological Survey (hereafter USGS), Trenton West Quadrangle (New Jersey-Pennsylvania) 1955, Photorevised 1981.

[4] Adam Hoops Executors to Thomas Barclay, April 30, 1773, Bucks County Deed Book 16, pp.226-228 and Deed of Sale from John Ashley et al, to Robert Morris, November 28, 1791, Bucks County Box, Historical Society of Pennsylvania.

[5] Benjamin Wood & wife to Adam Hoops, December 2, 1766, Bucks County Deed Book 15, pp.15-18 and Adam Hoops Executors to Thomas Barclay, April 31, 1773, Bucks county Deed Book 16, pp. 226-228.

SURVEYOR DESCRIPTIONS OF SUMMERSEAT PROPERTIES
Note: 1 perch = 16.5 feet, 1 chain = 66 feet

1764: Adam Hoops purchase
70 Acres plus Woods Island, described as 30 acres, purchased from Josiah Wood

Orientation		Perches	Feet	Code	Deed Narrative
S	65	W	252	4,158	A	- from creekside corner of Jabes Woods late land to a hickory tree
N	71	W	53.5	883	B	- to a stake in line of sd Jabes Wood Land
N	65	E	236	3,894	C	- to a stake by the Great Road side
N	29	W	24.5	404	D	- up the Great Road to stake at corner of orchard
N	57	E	47	776	E	- along row of apple trees to stake standing at other end of orchard
N	18	W	12	198	F	- to a stake
N	15	E	17.5	289	G	- to a Button Wood tree standing by the creek side
S		W				- back to the beginning

1765: Adam Hoops purchase
3 acres purchased from William Morris

Orientation			Chains	Feet	Code	Deed Narrative
						- from the Delaware River or Branch thereof which runs along the westerly side of Woods Island...along the Line of Josiah Woods' Land...to a post in said line
S	64	W	2	132	H	
S	43	E	16.3	1,076	I	- to a post
N	64	E	2.5	165	J	- to the said River
						- thence along the several courses therof to the place of Beginning

1766: Adam Hoops purchase
174 acres, purchased from Benjamin Wood

Orientation*			Perches	Feet	Code	Deed Narrative
S	65	W	224	3,696	K	- Beginning at a stone by the River Delaware at a corner of Land former George Biles's to a second stone for a corner
N	71.0	W	225	3,713	L	- to a third stone for a corner
N	15	W	48	792	M	- by land formerly Jeffrey Hawkins..to a stone set were (sic) formerly stood black oak marked for a corner
S	70	E	160	2,640	N	- by Josiah Woods Land to a hickory tree in the edge of a swamp
N	65	E	252	4,158	O	- to a black Oak standing near the bank of the sd River
S		W				- down the same several courses thereof to the Place of the Beginning

1773: Hoops Estate sale to Thomas Barclay ; also, 1791, Barclay (by Ashley) bankruptcy sale to Robert Morris
221.52 acres + small landing place 2.5 perches wide shared with Delaware Works

Orientation		Perches	Feet	Code	Match		Deed Narrative
S	65	W	228	3,762	i	K	-Begin at stone on River Del., corner ex-GeoBiles land
N	70.5	W	259.7	4,285	j	L	
N	18	W	48	792	k	M	-by land formerly of Jeffrey Hawkins to stone/ex-black oak
S	70.5	E	125.4	2,069	l	N	-by land formerly of Josiah Wood
N	65	E	242	3,993	m	C	
S	30	E	60	990	n	e	-by former Hoops land laid out for mill Lot, now of Robert Morris
S	15	E	21.84	360	o	d	
N	62	E	46.5	767	p	c	
S	35	E	21	347	q	b	
N	36.5	E	14.6	241	r	a	-to post on bank of creek/branch of River Delaware
							-back along the shoreline

*The 1766 deed for the 174 acres described the first and last segments of the tract boundary (above with codes K and O) as running West South West and East North East respectively. These are equivalent to S67.5W and N67.5E. For reasons described in the text, we are convinced that these are in error and should, in fact, be S65W and N65E respectively. The latter figures are used in the table and were used in mapping the property for presentation here.

Figure 1. Boundary definitions from deeds of 1764, 1765, 1766 and 1773

The segment codes are shown on the property outlines of the 70 and the 174 acre properties in Figure 2, marked by the upper case codes from the table of Figure 1. The 1773 border segments corresponding to segments defined in the earlier deeds are also shown in Figure 2, identified by lower case codes. Note the overlap of segments K and i, and L and j.   Figure 2 shows the relationship of the boundaries defined in the 1764 and 1766 deeds and those in the 1773 and later deeds.

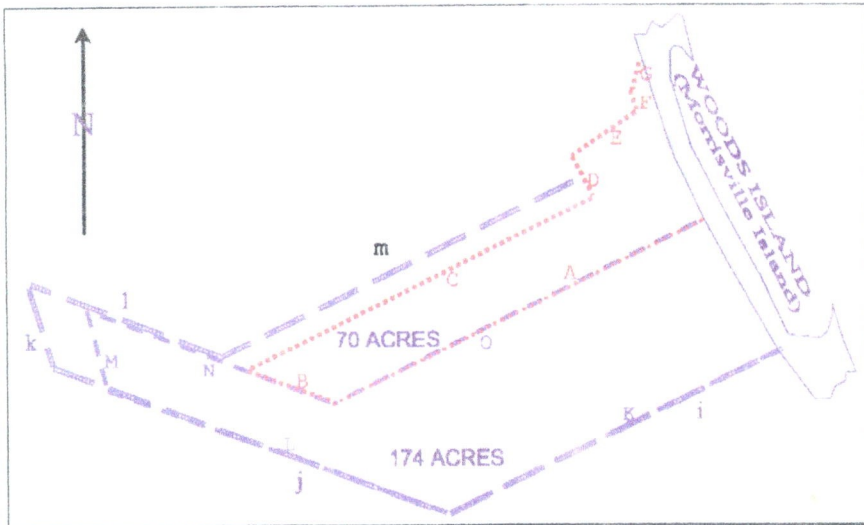

Figure 2. Comparison of tract boundaries as defined in 1764, 1766 and 1773 deeds

2. The second issue results from the fact that there is very little information in the deeds to fix the position of the plots along the bank of the Delaware and/or the creek between Woods Island (also called Morrisville Island) and the mainland on the maps. (This is particularly the case with the USGS map because the island no longer exists.)   Virtually all of the deed reference points defining the property are stakes, trees, rocks or the names of former or neighboring property owners, none of which appear on maps we have located.   The only useful exceptions are the starting point for each border definition, the riverbank (which has moved over the years) and a reference in the 1764 deed to land reserved for a school (in effect, an easement) which appears on some maps.[6]

3. The third issue is the location of the three acres bought by Adam Hoops in 1765. The only clue in the deed is that the land

---

[6] A reference to a segment of the border of the 70 acre plot that lies on "the great road" is interesting but not materially useful in positioning the property along the creek because this piece of border (and thus the road on which it lies) is roughly parallel with the creek bank.

border begins "at Delaware River or Branch thereof which runs along the westerly side of Woods Island" and ends "at the said River." [7]

Solutions

Definition of the overall border of the original Summerseat property. We have defined the original mainland Summerseat property on the basis of the border definition of the 1773 deed where the segments appear to correspond to those of the 1764 and 1766 deeds (i.e., segments i, j, k, l, m of the 1773 deed). Where they do not correspond, we used the 1764 deed as our source (segments D, E, F and G). The difference between this and ignoring the 1791 measurements is shown in Figure 3. It is this

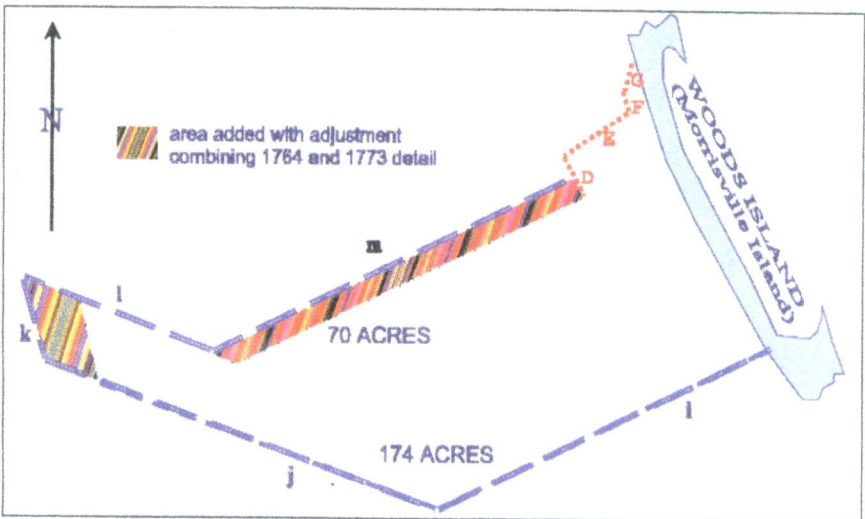

Figure 3. Adjusted borders of overall Summerseat property

adjusted overall border that is overlaid on the 1981 USGS map that appears in the text and in Figure 4 in this Appendix.[8]

This adjustment was supported by the following,

---

[7] William Morris & Wife to Adam Hoops, August 3, 1765, Bucks County Deed Book 11, pp.661-662.

[8] Thomas Barclay did not buy all of the Hoops land. The boundary of the piece he did buy turns southeast from the northeast end of segment "m." The segments of that boundary not shown in Figure 3 correspond more or less – but, here too, there are some anomalies - to those of land Hoops's estate sold to Richard Downing in April, 1773. Deed of Adam Hoops Executors to Richard Downing, April 10, 1773. Bucks County Box, Historical Society of Pennsylvania.

- The narrative descriptions of the plot corner markers and such identifying characteristics of border segments as the ownership of land along which they pass correspond from the 1766 deed to that of 1773, even when the measurements and/or compass directions are not identical.
- The description, including measurements and orientations, in the 1766 deed predates that deed, being identical with the description of land which Benjamin Wood mortgaged to Adam Hoops in March of 1765.[9] It may well come from a 1723 deed conveying the 174 acres from Joseph Wood to his son Jabus Wood, (who willed it to his son, Benjamin in 1759). In any case, there can be little doubt that the "West South West" orientation given in the 1766 deed (and the 1765 mortgage document) for boundary segment K and the parallel "East north East" for segment O are incorrect and should be S65W and N65E respectively, making them parallel with segments A and C of the 70 acres (overlapping in the case of A and O). The 1773 deed does show the orientation of segment K as S65W. We have used S65W and N65E for segments K and O in the table of Figure 1 and in all boundary outlines shown in the figures. This obvious inexactitude in the 1766 deed makes it easy to question measurements in the 1766 deed that differ from those of the 1773 document.
- The 1773 measurements were used in a subsequent transfer of ownership in 1791.
- No evidence has been found that Adam Hoops acquired additions to the initial plots that could explain the measurement differences in 1773 and 1791.
- Surveying tools and skills may have improved between 1764 and 1773.

Several facts make it clear that the 70 acres and the 174 acres were adjoining plots, which they would not be if the larger piece had been oriented WSW and the other W65W (a difference of 2.5°). .

- The deed for the 174 acres purchased from Benjamin Wood specifies that the land in question was inherited from his father, Jabus Wood; the description of the other plot, the 70 acres, has it beginning at "a corner of Jabes Woods late land."

- Boundary segments A and B of the 70 acres and N and O of the 174 acres have a common meeting point ("a hickory tree") and –

---

[9] Mortgage Deed, Benjamin Wood to Adam Hoops, March 20, 1765, Bucks County Deed Book 11, pp.336-337.

with the adjustment of segment O from WSW to S65W described above - matching orientations. (see Figures 1 and 2)

- The 1773 deed reflecting Thomas Barclay's purchase from Adam Hoops's estate encompasses both the 70 and 174 acres (albeit with some measurement differences, as discussed above).

Placing the Summerseat property on the map. The placement of the Summerseat land on available maps was based on the following information and assumptions:

- The boundaries of the 70 acres are described in the 1764 deed as "starting from creekside" and running to "a buttonwood tree standing by the creekside," thence back to the beginning.

- Although the corresponding language for the 174 acres in the 1766 deed is "beginning at a stone by the River Delaware" and "to a black oak standing near the bank of the sd River," the boundary clearly ends where the 70 acres start, which is on the creek, opposite Woods Island, not on the river. In addition, the 1766 purchase was described as "containing one hundred & seventy four Acres of Land Together with a small Landing Place on the sd River [the Delaware] of two perches and a half in Breadth joyning to the first mentioned Corner of the above Described Tract [the 174 acres]." Had the 174 acres included frontage on the River, this would have been unnecessary.

- In the 1764 deed for the 70 acres the property is defined as "Excepting and Preserving nevertheless one Half Acre of Land with the sd Bounds kept & Reseved (sic) for the Use of a school House".[10]   Both the main house on the Summerseat estate and the school house are shown on the 1876 map

.An unexpected problem arose when the property boundary overlay was oriented on the 1876 map by relating the surveyor directions of property border segments as found in the deeds to "North" as shown by the compass star on the map. With this approach, it was

---

[10] An 1813 deed between Henry L. Waddell and the Trustees of the Union School (Bucks County Deed Book 42, p.150) tells us that the half acre of land was set aside for the school in December 1762 by Josiah Wood. We do not have dimensions of this half acre in 1764, but the 1813 deed describes it as having grown to "thirteen twentieths" (0.65) acres. The length and orientation of three of its sides are given in deeds of 1812 (Henry Clymer to Wilson for Waddell; Bucks County Deed Book 41, pp.234-236) and 1860 (William Fetters and wife [the former Elizabeth Waddell] to Osborne; Bucks County Deed Book 111 pp.1-9).

impossible to get both the north and south waterfront limits of the property reasonably close to the water. This problem was resolved when the 1876 map was closely compared with the 1981 USGS map of the same area using digital copies of both maps. This revealed that North on the older map was approximately 8° east of North on the USGS map. When the property outline was turned 8°, it fit relatively easily on the 1876 map. Using the combination of the two maps (since only the older one actually shows the schoolhouse reference point), the outline was also placed on the 20th century map, as seen in Figure 1 in the text.

It seems reasonable to assume that Josiah Wood, the original grantor of the school easement in 1762, would have put it at the edge of his land. Indeed, when the plot outline, drawn to scale, using the measurements and orientations shown in the deeds, is placed on the 1876 map that shows the school house (once orientation problems described above were resolved), the school house does fall near the border of the 70 acres. This is shown in Figure 4.

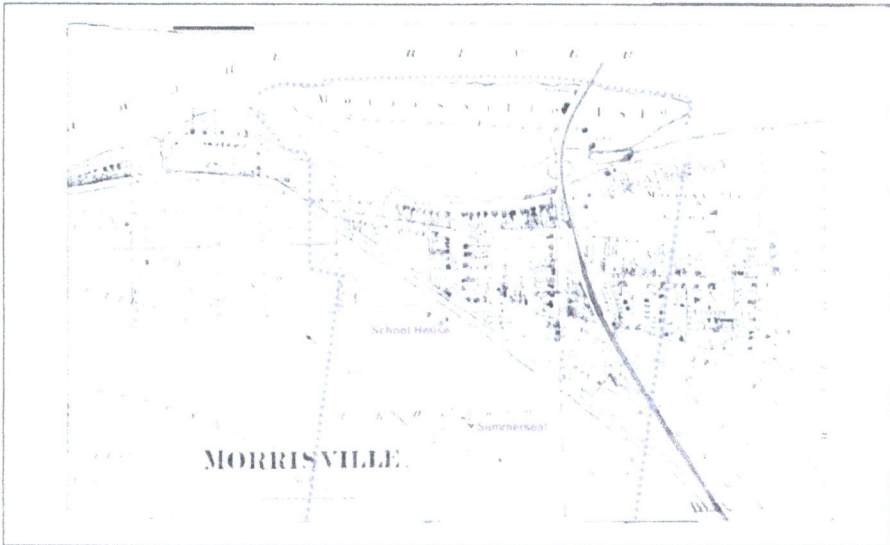

Figure 4. Summerseat property on an 1876 map of Morrisville Borough. The light blue line to the right of the school house is where the 70 acres and the 174 acres meet.

In addition to the above, there exists a Delaware Canal map from approximately 1836-1838 showing the Morrisville area in some

detail.[11]   Because of its level of detail and the fact that its origins
were closer to the period of Summerseat's development than the
1876 map, we wanted to overlay the outline of the property on it.
Working with digitized copies of this map on the computer, as we
did with the others, we found that there were significant differences
between the c.1836-1838 map and the later ones, while the two
later maps (USGS of 1981 and the 1876 map in Figure 5) are
mutually consistent.   As a result of this comparison, we concluded
that on the c.1836-1838 map the island, the school house and
Summerseat (labeled Waddell House for the then-current owner)
appear to be incorrectly located relative to one another and the
canal. Given these problems, we abandoned the idea of overlaying
the Summerseat property outline on this map.

The location of the three acres purchased in 1765._ The deed places
the three acres on the "Delaware River or Branch thereof which
runs along the westerly side of Woods Island" and provides the
orientation and length of the three inland sides. (see Figure 1)   We
have concluded that the three acres were on the creek shore where
the 174 acre tract meets the 70 acre tract bought from Josiah Wood
in 1764.   This conclusion is based on the following:

• The first leg of three acre tract boundary is described as
  "running along the Side of Josiah Woods' Land".

• That first leg runs South 64° West; the side of the 70 acres
  Hoops bought from Josiah Woods begins with a leg running
  South 65° West.

• There is an earlier (1765) reference to this land in the deed with
  which Benjamin Wood mortgaged to Hoops the 174 acres that
  Hoops would subsequently acquire. In that document, the
  boundaries of the 174 acres are defined in the exact same words
  as are found in the 1766 Wood/Hoops deed, except that, in the
  mortgage deed the description is "Excepting and Reserving
  nevertheless out of this Present Grant Three Acres taken Off the
  North East [corner of] the herein Described Tract of land Solde

---

[11] Map of the Delaware Division of the Pennsylvania Canal...[MorrisVille, Bird's
or Morrisville Island, Moon's Island, Turnpike Road], n.d. [c.1836-1838]. RG-17,
Records of the Office of Land Records. Canal Commissoners Map Books, Book
No. 2, p.5 [Folio 4], Pennsylvania State Archives, Pennsylvania Historical and
Museum Commission, Harrisburg.

by the said Jabes Wood unto a certain William Morris...". [12]

It was from William Morris that Hoops bought the three acres in 1765.

This conclusion also explains the absence of any reference to the three acres in later documents. There was no reason to mention them because they are encompassed in the overall definition of the 174 acres. Where the mortgage document explicitly excludes them from the 174 acre tract, later deeds implicitly include them by simply describing the overall boundary.

---

[12] The microfilm of the mortgage document shows damage making unreadable a short bit of text between "North East" and "the herein before Described...". We conclude from the context as well as from the information we have about the location of the three acres and the syntax here that the "missing" words are "corner of".

INDEX

AH = Adam Hoops   TB = Thomas Barclay